BEST KIND

BEST KIND

NEW WRITING MADE IN NEWFOUNDLAND

EDITED BY ROBERT FINLEY

BREAKWATER
P.O. Box 2188, St. John's, NL, Canada, A1C 6E6
www.breakwaterbooks.com

Copyright © 2018 Rob Finley

LIBRARY AND ARCHIVES CANADA CATALOGUING IN PUBLICATION
Best kind : new writing made in Newfoundland / Robert Finley, editor.
ISBN 978-1-55081-716-4 (softcover)
1. Canadian essays (English)--Newfoundland and Labrador. 2. Canadian essays (English)--21st century. 3. Creative nonfiction, Canadian (English)-- Newfoundland and Labrador. I. Finley, Robert, 1957-, editor
PS8373.1.B488 2018   C814'.60809718   C2018-900378-2

The cover and back-cover design of *Best Kind* are an homage to the former Newfoundland Margarine Company.

ALL RIGHTS RESERVED. No part of this work covered by the copyright hereon may be reproduced or used in any form or by any means—graphic, electronic or mechanical—without the prior written permission of the publisher. Any request for photocopying, recording, taping or storing in an information retrieval system of any part of this book shall be directed in writing to Access Copyright, One Yonge Street, Suite 800, Toronto, Ontario, M5E 1E5.

We acknowledge the support of the Canada Council for the Arts, which last year invested $153 million to bring the arts to Canadians throughout the country. We acknowledge the financial support of the Government of Canada and the Government of Newfoundland and Labrador through the Department of Tourism, Culture, Industry and Innovation for our publishing activities.
PRINTED AND BOUND IN CANADA.

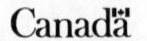

Breakwater Books is committed to choosing papers and materials for our books that help to protect our environment. To this end, this book is printed on a recycled paper that is certified by the Forest Stewardship Council®.

CONTENTS

ROBERT FINLEY Introduction... **7**

BRIDGET CANNING Questions and Answers on Flight and Butchery... **17**

JOHN ROBINSON BLACKMORE La respiration sacrée... **31**

EVA CROCKER Swimming Pools... **43**

DANIELLE DEVEREAUX Des biscuits... **51**

ELENA SLAWINSKA Pleasure and Other Nutritious Matters... **57**

AMY DONOVAN Night Walk... **73**

MATTHEW HOLLETT Painting the Curlew... **85**

JOAN SULLIVAN Clive Wearing Writes (and Writes and Writes) His Autobiography... **97**

IRENE VELENTZAS Hidden in Plain Sight... **111**

MICHELLE PORTER She Gets a Paper Route so She Can Save Up for a Bicycle... **131**

HEIDI WICKS Fireflies... **147**

PAUL WHITTLE A Sketch of Stephen... **159**

Acknowledgements... **171**

Contributors... **175**

INTRODUCTION

ROBERT FINLEY

Any given evening of winter, spring, summer, or fall, if you happen to be walking by the Arts Building on Memorial University's St. John's campus, stop for a minute and look up at the third-floor windows. The lights will be burning there. Outside, night is falling around you. Inside, a dozen people are gathered around a big table covered in coffee cups, papers, laptops, pens, and pencils. Three of them are leaning in, right on the edge of their chairs, one has pulled a leg up under her and is making notes, two others are slouched against their seat backs, hunkered down, brow-furrowed. One takes a sip of his coffee. Several people are speaking at once. There is some gesticulating going on. In a minute, laughter will break out—sustained, inclusive, consuming; or, it might be silence—a concentrated, collective silence; or, it might be spontaneous, heartfelt applause. They've been at it for a couple of hours already and they are far from done. They are talking about writing, its furthest reaches, its minutest particulars, and they are talking with the passionate engagement, precision, astonishment, and plain joy that the making of art calls for and calls forth. They are voluble, astute, and kind, and they are likely going over time.

Theirs is an ongoing conversation which lies at the heart of the creative-writing workshop process. All of the essays gathered in this collection have grown out of that process, written, workshopped, and revised by participants in Memorial University's Creative Writing Program over the past three years. All are utterly distinct in voice. Each, at the same time, forms part of what it is fair to call a collective enterprise—a program producing a constant, vital torrent of new work, of thought, of feeling, hundreds of finished pieces every year of poetry, fiction, playwriting, screenwriting, podcasting, and the essay.

The twelve essays in this book represent that larger collective and substantially collaborative enterprise of which they are a part. They have also been chosen for what they have to say, taken together, about this wonderful, varied, open, inclusive, old and new form of writing: the essay. With origins far older than the sixteenth century, the form takes its name from Michel de Montaigne's 1580 publication of his *Essais*—a book of "trials" or "attempts," "tests" or "experiments." The word comes into English as both *essay* and *assay*, both terms Montaigne would likely find apt translations of his French, as he speaks of his book as a series of attempts to get the measure of his own thinking, to assay the self by writing. "*Que sais-je?*" he asks.

INTRODUCTION

"What do I know?" It is a question probably safe to enunciate on Montaigne's behalf, both earnestly and with a shrug of the shoulders, palms turned upward, eyebrows raised. John D'Agata calls the form "the equivalent of a mind in rumination, performing as if improvisationally the reception of new ideas, the discovery of unknowns, the encounter with the 'other.'" It is also a form written almost exclusively in the first-person singular, and because of this has sometimes been taken to task for being self-indulgent, or too inwardly focused. This is partly the fault of Montaigne himself, who begins his 1580 volume with a charming if slightly disingenuous note, "To the Reader":

> This, reader, is an honest book. It warns you at the outset that my sole purpose in writing it has been a private and domestic one… I am myself the substance of my book, and there is no reason why you should waste your leisure on so frivolous and unrewarding a subject. Farewell then, from Montaigne, this first day of March, 1580.

Two lines into Montaigne's book, however, readers have been discovering for over five hundred years that if the objective of Montaigne's essays is to assay the self, they do so by looking outward: Montaigne's *I* is first and foremost an *I-witness* attending to the world through the lens of personal experience and alive to what the nineteenth century essayist Alexander Smith calls, "the infinite suggestiveness of common things." In her introduction to the 2017 *Best American Essays*, Leslie

Jamison's word for this is *encounter*. "To me," she says, "the essay's defining trait is the situation and problem of encounter… whether you are regarding the self, the world, the past, the other, the other's mother, the vacant lot next door, the transatlantic flight, the dry cleaners, the burlesque. The essay inherently stages an encounter between an 'I' and the world in which that 'I' resides."

The encounters you will encounter here in these pages include encounters with darkness, the body, a midnight moose, with memory and its absence, with a shared sinister pairing on your DNA, with the corporation, the beloved, with loss, with lunch, with a single, lustrous fig newton, with the altered gravity of trauma, the public swimming pool, sex, an extinct species, with a psychiatric ward, fireflies, the self, and the wide, wide world. Each of these encounters takes its own shape. In "The Essay as Form," Theodore Adorno offers what is perhaps the finest description of the form's basic structure: in the essay, he says,

> Thought does not advance in a single direction, rather the aspects of the argument interweave as in a carpet. The fruitfulness of the thoughts depends on the density of this texture. Actually, the thinker does not think, but rather transforms himself into an arena of intellectual experience without simplifying it… the essay… proceeds, so to speak, methodically unmethodically.

INTRODUCTION

The authors included in this book push at the borders of the form, explore its limits, extend its rangy possibilities, define it…through practice—each a locus for experience with their own strengths and preoccupations. Each of their essays is a unique strategy for attending to complexity, a search for a form that accommodates without simplifying.

In "Flight and Butchery," Bridget Canning strings five taut scenes, discontinuous in time but tonally aligned. Then she sets them ringing together, drawing out of them a resonance, a presence, "an encompassing protective light." In "*La respiration sacrée*," John Blackmore takes up the first in a series of portraits of individual friends and acquaintances. Luminous in its particulars, its language is playful and precise and edged with irony and empathy both. "This is where you learn what's in store for you," says Eva Crocker in "Swimming Pools," writing with a clarity and an attention to the human form through its ages that betokens love.

"Be light like a bird, not a feather," admonishes Italo Calvino in his *Six Memos for the New Millennium*, quoting Paul Valery. All of the pieces in this book realize qualities of directed and intentional lightness. Look, for example, to Danielle Devereaux's "*Des biscuits*," where the weight of the world is for a moment sweetly set aside by a single, necessary, and timely fig newton; or to Elena Slawinska's "Pleasure and Other Nutritious Matters," which invites us to sit *a tavola* through a long Ligurian afternoon and enjoy the most sparkling, convivial, and extended cultural practice of an Italian lunch.

W.G. Sebald describes the essay as a walking form, inquisitive, nimble, grounded, and ready to pause and consider:

> As you walk along you find things by the wayside, or you buy a brochure written by a local historian…and in that you find odd details that lead you somewhere else…it's a form of unsystematic searching… and as they have been assembled in this random fashion, you have to strain your imagination in order to create a connection between things…you have to take heterogeneous materials in order to get your mind to do something that it hasn't done before.

Amy Donovan and Matthew Hollett likewise approach the essay on foot. In "Night Walk" Amy uses her own skin, her own hearing, sense of smell and taste and touch to think about the creaturely presences and perspectives that surround her during a night walk through the sensuous darkness of the Cape Breton Highlands. And Matthew wanders through the specimen vaults at The Rooms, Kijiji, the writings of John James Audubon, and other literature relating to the eskimo curlew, in his thoughtful, spacious meditation on the eternal nap of extinction, our own included. Michelle Porter's "She Gets a Paper Route so She Can Save Up for a Bicycle," on the other hand, is a searing compression of time and circumstance so tightly and intelligently plotted it is impossible to look away

INTRODUCTION

from the page and what it threatens. Joan Sullivan adapts documentary theatre techniques in an essay constructed entirely of quoted passages from discrete sources. These she sets into conversation with each other to weave a net of care beneath the desperate high-wire act of Clive Wearing's autobiography-without-memory. Irene Velentzas also invokes memory in "Hidden in Plain Sight" to come to an understanding of two central passionate attachments of her life, one personal, one professional. Paul Whittle, in his tender, careful, clear-sighted "A Sketch of Stephen," takes us into the troubling world of a mental-health unit through a narrative reconstruction of his time working there through one season in the mid-eighties. And in "Fireflies," Heidi Wicks, with her fluency in the essay's language of particulars, takes us to one summer evening in the New Hampshire woods and the cusp of adolescence in a piece that is funny, and charming, and sharp enough to cut.

For Leslie Jamison, "The essay works in moments of disruption. It lives in the belief that no beauty is innocent, no ugliness fixed or simple, every life is bottomless, and no experience is ever only private. An essay doesn't simply transcribe the world, it finds the world." Reader, here you will find a little of the world of our evenings under a fluorescent hum in the Arts Building…winter, spring, summer, or fall…the lights are burning there right now. And you will find twelve writers committed to bearing witness to the wider world in all its difficulty, complexity, its strangeness and beauty. Their gift to us through each encounter is to teach us again and again to let go of what we thought we knew, to relinquish our certainties, to wonder.

Endless thanks are due the folks at Breakwater for taking this project on and giving it voice; to my wonderful colleague Lisa Moore, source of every good thing, whose *Racket: New Writing Made in Newfoundland* has been the model and inspiration for this collection; to the students and faculty of Memorial University's Creative Writing Program, all of whom have a hand in what happens here; and, of course, to the writers themselves for their generous gifts.

QUESTIONS AND ANSWERS ON FLIGHT AND BUTCHERY

BRIDGET CANNING

At age eleven, I witness my father send someone airborne. I won't know why for sixteen years. We are in Placentia for a family reunion. Eight of my father's brothers return to the province with their partners and kids. The girls are outnumbered: eight of us out of twenty cousins. And Gran and Pop had only sons. There was one daughter who died in infancy, then eight boys, then twins, both boys. Would you like a side of boys with those boys? The ten sons made twenty grandchildren and still only eight girls out of the lot.

We are at Uncle Joseph's house on a warm August evening. There has been a barbeque, homemade cookies, and glasses of pop. My cousins and I are beside the front steps. There are various toys and sidewalk chalk. The adults occupy the kitchen. Sometimes, someone emerges to make sure we aren't killing each other.

BEST KIND

The girl cousins get along well despite age differences. Genevieve is fifteen with spiky hair and mismatched earrings and she says wearing my slouch socks over the cuffs of my jeans looks dumb. But most of the time she is nice. My cousin Olivia is two years younger than me and forbidden to eat processed sugar. Her dad, Joseph, hasn't eaten red meat since he was a teenager. He juices vegetables and mixes them with liquid green chlorophyll purchased in large white jugs from health-food stores. He chugs a full glass after breakfast and pours me some in a little shot glass. It's getting all your vegetables at once, he says. It tastes like potting soil—clean, but still dirt.

Olivia's parents have warned all the local shopkeepers not to sell her candy. But my sister and I are unknown in Placentia stores. Olivia roots for loose change under couch cushions and skims dimes from coin jars. She presses them into my palm and whispers her desires: Kraft caramels. Swedish berries. Double Bubble. I drop her stash in her right bunny slipper. When she has blue jawbreaker teeth, I signal that she should brush them. It's funny, but she's all rapid speech and giggles afterwards and she makes me tired.

Olivia wants Tootsie Rolls and Cousin Chris overhears. He says he's going to tell if I don't get him some too. This is what is happening when the two strange men stroll up the path and enter the house. They walk with long loping steps with cigarettes in their mouths. They open the door and sing out to Uncle Clarence. Their voices are lifted greetings in the porch,

QUESTIONS AND ANSWERS ON FLIGHT AND BUTCHERY

unanswered by voices inside.

We forget about them until the front door opens again. The surprised, protesting head of a man emerges, level with the doorknob. It makes me think the body is levitating, like in a magician's act. The head withdraws and reappears with its accompanying carcass. The man sails over the steps and plops on the concrete walk.

We freeze. My father appears holding the second man, gripping the seat of his pants and jean-jacket collar. His arms and legs dangle like a kitten carried in its mother's mouth. Dad hurls him over the steps with a heave-ho rhythm; he lands like a pile of wet string. The two blue-denim heaps curse and moan. They scramble off, the fence latch banging.

I follow Dad into the house; my cheeks puffed out with questions.

Dad, why did you do that?

They were rude.

I follow him into the kitchen. His back is a straight, calm line. Uncle Cletus hands him a beer. I take big steps to get around the front of Dad and gape up at him.

What happened?

No answer. He takes a few peanuts from a bowl and offers them to me. I don't want any peanuts.

Oh, those two? Uncle Cletus says. They had to go.

He smiles. They all do, all my adult relatives smile with a special light. The ice cubes in their glasses nudge each other knowingly. For two days, my cousins and I ask what happened, but the topic gets changed or a question is asked in response. Like they are an exclusive club with their own secret, untouchable amusements.

At age fourteen, I am sent airborne and I know why.

Grade nine is not the year to cross me. Every day is black eyeliner day. The people you want to talk to never do, and the people you hate never leave you alone. You'd think they'd know better.

Mike shoves his sweatshirt sleeves as far up his arm as possible to create the illusion of biceps. He looks more like Olive Oyl with puffed sleeves. He walks with a practiced swagger so his knees bounce out, marionette style. His eyes have sleep crusties and his hair has dandruff flakes which I am forced to look at because Mrs. Gilliam makes me sit behind him. Mrs. Gilliam says in grade nine, students shouldn't need a seating arrangement, but we give her no choice. She separates the pairs of friends, the mutually attracted, and the boys. Mike has a front seat so she can keep an eye on him; I am nearsighted and next.

Mike enjoys turning slightly like he's looking at the board and messing with whatever he can reach on my desk: pushing a pencil onto the floor, elbowing my eraser off the edge.

Pick it up.
No.
Pick it up.

QUESTIONS AND ANSWERS ON FLIGHT AND BUTCHERY

If Becky sees, he picks it up—Becky is scary. If Christa sees, he picks it up—Christa is pretty. In grade eight, Mike smiled at me all the time, but this memory now embarrasses him. Or maybe he was nice last year because Dad was dying. Which is just like everyone else, all questions and pity gone now. No one asks anything. No one says stomach cancer. And every time I remember last year and returning Mike's smiles and thinking he had cute dimples, I dig my fingernails into my palms to punish myself. I would really like to hit Mike.

It is the third week of January. Three months until Easter break; everyone prays for snow days or for the furnace to bust so school will close. But at home, we all wait to feel better and the refrigerator humming is the loudest sound.

On this day, I go with Mom to school and get there early. When I enter the classroom, only Mike and Neil are there. My binder is on the floor. Loose-leaf sheets fan out across the tiles—a pack of 500, on sale at Woolco. Assholes. I know Mike did it.

Pick up my binder, Mike.

No way.

Pick it up.

Fuck you, bitch.

I step forward and his jean-jacket collar is wadded in my fist.

Pick it up.

His palms flat on my shoulders. He pushes back.

Fuck off.

He walks off in his stupid, bouncy strut. Neil cackles behind me. The back of my hand slashes across Mike's head with its dirty, uncombed curls. He turns. I push. He pushes. I slap him in the face. He pushes me away. My foot out—he knows what I'm going for. And I fly backwards, my spine slides across a desk, desk falls over, books on floor. My side kills. Neil laughs in high, shocked squeals.

I make it to the girls' washroom without crying. Nicole is there; she's in grade eleven and when I tell her what happened, she says Mike is a fucking pussy. I wait until the bell rings to return to class. Everyone can see my puffy eyes. My binder is on my desk. The back of Mike's ears are pink. He doesn't turn around.

At age nine, I watch my father slice open a lamb. We aren't allowed to watch them get killed, but it's impossible not to see them already dead. On our farm, there is always something dead and at least three kinds of shit on the ground.

I sit on the top rail of the fence near the post because I know this is the strongest spot. It is late afternoon and the sky is a saucer of milk. The lamb is headless and upside down. Blood drips into a bucket under the neck hole. The bucket is almost full.

Why do you only kill the boys?

Because we only need two rams and we already have Malcolm and Cyril.

Dad wears the hat Mom knit him pulled over his ears. He runs a knife back and forth on a whetting stone. He has a few

QUESTIONS AND ANSWERS ON FLIGHT AND BUTCHERY

knives, one is like a hook. He slits the lamb open with a long slash through the middle and another straight down the front, like the sign of the cross.

Why do you cut it that way?

It's easier to get at the organs.

Dad pulls back the skin flaps. Things fall out. The parts inside are red, pink, blue, purple, and white. He points with the hooked knife and says their names: intestines, liver, bladder.

Where's the heart?

Here.

Dad displays the heart on the end of the curved knife. It is rounded and smooth, like a beach rock.

I make no noise while I watch. Boys in my class whoop and bray when they talk about blood and guts. They have to make noise whenever they do anything: walking into a room, getting their books out. Like Gregory on the bus, going on about his new skidoo to no one in particular. A Yamaha. Brand new. Some power. Who cares? I know he faints at the sight of blood.

Go back now. Tell your mother I'll be forty-five minutes.

The sea looks stony and secret behind the house. I feel puffed up for not getting grossed out. The only part that surprised me was the sound of guts falling on grass. Shuck-shuck.

At age thirty-seven, I get sliced open. Before it happens, I get really scared twice. First, during the meeting with the nurse who talks about my DNA and preventative surgery for those with the risk of hereditary diffuse gastric cancer. She lists statistics. When she produces the brochure for prophylactic gastrectomy, I snatch her box of tissues.

Oh my dear, she says. You help yourself.

Next is on the gurney. There are two others waiting, an old man with a concave chest and scraps of hair like chicken feathers and a bald woman with tubes in her nose. She gnaws the inside of her cheeks. We are all waiting for procedures; we have all been tagged and prepped.

I choke on panic sobs as they wheel me into the operating room. It is the brightest, whitest room I've ever seen. Swingy big-band music plays and everyone wears colourful masks and caps. The nurse I met earlier peers at me; her cap is the Union Jack.

Oh Sweetie, don't worry.

I'm sorry. I can't stop crying.

Gawd, if it was me, I'd be screechin'.

Everyone bounces subtly to the music. It is the most hygienic dance party ever. This is calming; employees that like their work should be good at it. Union Jack Nurse notices I'm still wearing my underwear.

You have to have everything off under your robe.

I started my period this morning.

Oh maaan, that sucks.

A nurse with Smurfs on her cap shakes her head at this:

QUESTIONS AND ANSWERS ON FLIGHT AND BUTCHERY

You poor thing. Like you don't have enough going on. We'll remove your underwear while you're out.

They say lean way forward and the epidural is liquid ice on the base of my spine. They say count back from ten. I get to eight.

The nurse says my name. Time to wake up. She rubs my arms to warm them. I would like to sleep more, but it's time to wake up. This takes a while. When I'm lucid, I am pushed out into the ward. Mom, Liz, Jason, and Jon are there. They speak in raised octaves and say gentle things like there she is, and hiiiii. I ask what time it is. Almost 6pm. I went under at eight. The surgery took over eight hours because the stomach expands and it's hard to get it all. Jon didn't leave the hospital the entire time.

There is a neo-nasal tube in my nose. There is an oxygen tube under my nostrils and across my face. There is an IV tube in my left hand. There is a feeding tube in the left side of my abdomen so they can still feed me if there's infection. There is a draining tube opposite it with a tentacle-like pink rubber sack which fills up with horror water. Apparently, there is a catheter. I can't feel it. There is a thick blue maxi pad between my legs.

I haven't told many people. Uncle Brian has ranted: Don't tell people about our genetic issues; it's like we're some fucking biological experiment. I send emails to say the surgery went okay. My friend Justin texts to see how I am and I text that I'm hooked up like the Borg and he thinks this is really funny.

The first night, the other women in the ward are like pre-teens at a slumber party. They watch *So You Think You Can Dance*, with the volume jacked. The woman behind the right curtain makes observant commentary: that's what you call The Very Sexual Dancing. I look at Jon and mouth I hate her.

But I hate the neo-nasal tube the most. It tugs and pinches when I move and I am never unaware of this stiff rod in my face, like a dead trout on a carrying stick. And no fluids until they're sure the surgery was successful. I encircle my mouth with wet blue sponges on lollipop sticks, but they bring only momentary relief. I always need to have them in reach. I am a chain-sponger.

Day three, I am brought into X-ray and drink orange-pink barium. It tastes like liquid chalkboard dust with some Tang crystals dumped in. I have to hold myself up for the X-ray. It is hard to stand. Tubes and wires dangle and I am a salvaged boat dragged up from the seafloor, dripping in the tangle of its own gear.

Later, in the ward, I am told everything is fine. The nurse unlatches the tape keeping in the bastard neo-nasal tube and yanks it from my face in one motion. My sinuses wail in raw relief. Then she gives me a pineapple popsicle. I love her.

Day four, I poop and I'm so excited because it means my insides work and I can get the fuck out of the hospital soon. I text friends to tell them about my poop. I'm out on day six, but

QUESTIONS AND ANSWERS ON FLIGHT AND BUTCHERY

the feeding tube has to stay in for thirty days. Three times a day, I plunge water into it with a large plastic syringe, to keep it clear. I can feel the cold water I push into my own intestine.

There is little space between my esophagus and small intestine. It will stretch, but at first I can only eat small portions of food. For months, I regularly spit up the excess. Jon gets used to me silently rising from the table and rushing from the room. I lose thirty-seven pounds. I try to write, but everything is work. Getting up is work, drinking water is work, driving is work, work is the worst work. I sleep like I'm made of wood and I remember no dreams for over seven months. I complain about it and feel like an asshole; I have done this to myself. But keeping my stomach was a game of Russian roulette. Dad, Cletus, and Clarence are gone. Everyone is glad I've done this.

At age twenty-seven, I find out. I am at Uncle Joseph's Christmas party:

So, what happened?

Oh, they were locals; they went to high school with Clarence. They'd been drinking all day when they crashed the party. No one could stand them. They wouldn't shut up.

What made Dad snap?

Your sister walked in. I guess she was eleven or twelve? She got a drink from the fridge and left. When she was gone, one of them made a remark about her ass.

What a tool.

Derm said nothing. Put his drink down, picked them up and flung them out the door. Always forgot how strong he was. He took a zero-tolerance approach to that comment.

I nod. I put ice cubes in my drink so they crack, fizzing and excited. Topics change. Olivia is home from BC; my sister is engaged. I excuse myself. In the bathroom, I sit on the tub and take deep breaths. I can't get upset. I've had enough to drink to go from pleasantly tipsy to maudlin. But how many bad boyfriends and rude dates might have ended up treated with the same fierceness and gallantry.

Or not. Maybe I'd still have taken care of myself.

I close the bathroom door and return to the kitchen. Supper dishes have been dealt with, candles lit, music on. My extended family extends across the room, teasing, telling stories. All in a dialect of contagious laughter. All under an encompassing, protective light.

LA RESPIRATION SACRÉE

JOHN ROBINSON BLACKMORE

Salomé's stilettos clack and snap as her standard-issue red high heels make their way across the pavement toward Emirates Headquarters, adjacent to Dubai International.

The freshly paved streets lack the cracks and erosion of her home in Saint-Pierre. At fourteen, on her way to school, in the midst of winter, she often trekked through the unprofitable Collectivité d'Outre-mer wearing heels. The impracticality had nothing to do with vanity or aspirations of presenting herself as mature. She knew she needed the practice in order to manifest her destiny as a flight attendant.

In Dubai, her boyfriend, Nakul, has taken the afternoon off work. He will pick her up when her meeting is over. As to where they will go, he replies, "Doesn't matter."

Salomé holds down the audio record on WhatsApp. "I cannot talk right now. I am almost eenside…What are you saying, eet *doesn't matter*? You don't theenk what happened to me was serious? Or eet doesn't matter eef you see me, you don't geeve a fuck"—she sighs deeply—"you don't geeve a sheet eef you see me before I leave again, tomorrow."

Inside HQ she identifies herself to security. Swarms of red hats from which white scarfs are draped to frame faces of all ethnicities mirror Salomé's own appearance, including her desert-brown jacket and red skirt. Men are clean-cut with matching suits and ties. Behind a counter, one of them tells her to take a seat while she awaits her meeting with a general manager. She doesn't know how long she'll be waiting, or whether or not she'll get time off to recuperate at her grandmother's in France. The uncertainty is something she's habituated to.

Nearly three years ago in Lyon, over a thousand people assembled for the Emirates recruitment session. Rounds of questions and group activities while under careful observation whittled the number down to hundreds. No feedback was ever given. The first personal interaction with the hiring staff came when the hundreds were culled to five. Once again, these interviews were completed without any feedback. At the day's end, the five became four and the four were instructed to await the possibility of a Golden Call in subsequent months.

Four months of waiting for an inevitability. Salomé had asked her higher self for the job, had consulted her clairvoyant guide about whether she was going to be hired. And plus, not only did she rock the day of testing, fuming with charisma and charm, she had put a jade egg *dans son vagine. Les vibrations étaient juste parfait.* She had no trouble visualizing herself meeting interesting people and seeing the world; it was crystal clear.

Her phone pings with a Facebook message from her mother, simultaneously and subconsciously pinging memories from when Salomé was sixteen: "*Espèce de pute qui lèche les chattes. Salope.*"

These comments weren't spoken from what was normally an ethereal maternal presence. If Salomé's psyche were a web, it held enough tangled traumas, *grâce à maman*, to nourish any baby spider's appetite.

Uninterested in reading the latest bland stroke of grey, aiming to create a picture of lustrous life updates between mother and daughter, Salomé closes her eyes to reflect on the story that brought her here. She hasn't even prepared what she is going to say.

Salomé prepared to work a roundtrip from Dubai to Colombo, Sri Lanka. The computer system at HQ notified her she was due for her weekly blood test. She queued with a line of co-workers whose names she may never learn. Though they all adorned the mandatory mascara, eyeliner, eyebrow pencil, foundation, blush, and red lipstick, they were never likely to share a cabin in the sky. Emirates had over 35,000 cabin crew—less than half of the total 75,000 the company employed.

BEST KIND

On board the Boeing 747, Salomé made her way up and down the aisles, helping passengers, eventually coming to her galley—a small cut-out space with cupboards, near two toilets—of which she was the "operator" for this flight.

In preparation for her colleague's seatbelt etc. announcement, she took out her iPhone to switch to airplane mode—ignoring all alerts except Nakul's, sending "*bisous bisous* ox" to him before takeoff.

Many of her Indian customers were arrogant, but Nakul wasn't a self-entitled, wealthy ex-pat. His father fixed air conditioners. He left Chennai's familiar scene for Dubai and its constant need for machines that churn desert air into modern mirages—artificial oases from the searing sun. Nakul followed suit with most of his countrymen in choosing to study software engineering. These days he was on hiatus, working for Dad.

"She ees my mother. You know? Eet is sacred." She had inhaled, then huffed, "Or, eet ees something. I know. But…"

Nakul had sat up from his supine position.

"Eet's just, I don't know. Obviously, my mother. I would be sad, maybe. *Mais, en fait*…I theenk, maybe, I wood be happy-are for her to start a new life, you know?"

"New life where?" he had asked.

"Like, you know, a new birth. Obviously, I don't wish death on her," she had said quickly. "Eet's just, eef she ees causing thees much suffering, she must suffer eenside too."

LA RESPIRATION SACRÉE

Salomé tried to create intimacy, sharing bits of her life when she could. A work schedule without definite days off, and two in a row being rare. Often she found herself rising above the clouds, towards a new city, where invariably there would be interesting people to meet.

Salomé's galley had two empty food carts, used and unopened trays on the counter, cleaning supplies scattered about, tissue boxes and paper towel at the ready. Nearby, passengers were lined up for the bathroom. The same gentleman who had been at the front when she began eating tomato sauce and noodles was still standing in queue.

She poked her head out of the galley, "Everytheeng alright?"

The man first in line shuffled from one foot to the other. His hand hung loosely near his pocket, gently tapping his leg. He smiled his assurance that everything was fine.

After finishing her two clementines and a banana, the line still hadn't moved.

"Eet has been a while, no? A long wait?"

An exhale and raised eyebrows confirmed as much. She moved past the small group, and politely rapped on the bathroom door.

No response.

She knocked with more force. "Allo? Ees everytheeng alright?"

Once again, no response.

"Perhaps eet weel be better to use the bathroom just across the aisle." Salomé pointed to the other side of the plane with her corporate smile. The passengers disbursed. She lifted the metallic "lavatory" sign on the door. Her view was limited, but nobody was sitting on the toilet. She reached inside to unlock the door—it wouldn't push open. The door needed to fold inward before closing into the wall. Something was preventing the fold from happening.

Salomé knew what was waiting for her. Panic was as far away as the cold, windy rock she called home. There was no ignoring what laid before her. She reassured herself that she was meant to be there on that flight for this purpose.

She paged Harsha, her Purser, told him he might need an axe, and went to tidy her galley. Everything needed to be stowed, and the carts removed to make space for the procedure.

Two doctors and two nurses responded to the request for a medical professional over the PA. They converged in Salomé's galley with Harsha.

The man who lay on a stretcher before them was named John. He was wearing a short-sleeve blue shirt and jeans, aged seventy-two.

His face lacked all trace of colour. The ferry home from Fortune often rolled its way over feisty North Atlantic swells, and John was looking worse than the many passengers—Salomé had witnessed countless times—who vomited in the complimentary paper bags.

LA RESPIRATION SACRÉE

Protocol states an employee must attempt resuscitation on any unconscious passenger, for at least forty-five minutes.

"There's no point," said the UK doctor. "He is, without a doubt, dead."

Harsha said, "Let me page the captain."

"Not much in his seat," An American cabin-crew member said, turning the corner. "Only this." He held up a book, *Modesty Blaise*.

Harsha returned to Salomé. "They understand the situation, but protocol is in place to protect us from liability issues."

Salomé nods. "I weel gheeve air?"

Harsha removed his vest, rolled his sleeves, finicked with them, "Nothing you can do?" he asked the doctor.

"He's not with us anymore," she replied.

Harsha began pumping John's chest. After thirty, Salomé placed a rubber mask-like device over John's mouth—another part of protocol. Several years ago, a flight attendant attempted to resuscitate a passenger, and some blood was coughed up. She was dutifully performing mouth to mouth without a plastic guard, and for her lifesaving efforts, she contracted HIV.

John's eyes were closed. There was no smell in particular, no decay other than the absence of skin colour.

As Harsha pumped and Salomé pressed her lips to plastic, she would only think about what he was going to miss. Did he know about the solar flash? The pending ascension? Alien contact, and upgraded technologies that are soon-to-be unsuppressed?

It's a good thing his life didn't depend on the CPR because Harsha consistently stopped pumping, obviously flummoxed, to ask something stupid like, "Do you know the cause of death?"

A white foamy liquid seeped out of John's mouth. Salomé assumed (and hoped) it was saliva as she wiped it away, again and again.

Harsha had cracked a couple ribs. John's chest was heavily bruised. Purple, black, blue, red—olive tea colours.

Harsha once again stopped mid-pump to ask if the doctors would like some water.

C'est quoi cette merde? There's twenty-six letters een the alphabet, water can exeest een three different states, there's no avoiding taxes, we all exeest because of our mother, and there are no eenterruptions when performing CPR. How can he be een charge of all these staff and passengers eef he can't do hees fucking job!

She lowered to John's lips, futilely, dutifully, obligatorily trying to breathe life into his corpse.

At HQ, Salomé opens her messenger to respond to her mother. As her thumb hovers over the touch screen, a hand touches her shoulder.

"We're ready for you now," says a sultry Australian accent. "Salomé, right?"

LA RESPIRATION SACRÉE

"Yes!" She quickly stows her phone in her purse.

The general manager is not on site, and Salomé finds herself in front of a desk phone on speaker. A prissy British voice informs her that a passenger's death, no matter how traumatic the experience might be, doesn't warrant any vacation time.

"I can take weethout pay, eef eets necessary," says Salomé.

"I'm sorry but I must reiterate that your request is unmerited. I know your recent shift must have been tasking, and I have to say that we're glad to have you uphold Emirates' exemplary customer service." There was nothing to do but pack for Bangkok the following day.

At home, she inspects her uniform extra closely, looking for any spit shrapnel or uncomely stains. For the first time she realizes her heels are worn out. The sides are scuffed, the bottoms are filthy, and the support is going to cave at any moment.

Her dream is nearly three years old, and what has it brought her? Apart from authentic recipes, clothing, and casual sex with every ethnicity but Korean, this latest incident highlighted her need for something steadier than a bedside table covered in crystals.

Nakul's knock on her apartment door interrupts her train of thought. She can't remember why she didn't call him for a ride when she left HQ. Whatever the reason was, her flight leaves in less than twelve hours, she knows they will let it slide.

SWIMMING POOLS

EVA CROCKER

HOW TO HOLD YOUR BREATH

My mother taught me to swim when I was an infant by flinging me off the wharf into the pond she grew up on. Or that's what I believed for a long time. Really she stood hip deep in the pond and lowered me slowly in and out of the water, awakening something already inside me; how to hold my breath and churn my limbs. Somewhere along the way, I contorted that story into one where my mother dropped me off the wharf, full of faith that I would paddle back up to the surface, and I came through for her.

GADBOIS COMMUNITY CENTER, MONTREAL

A gangly boy who looks about eight is climbing the ladder to the diving board. He yells to his brother in Spanish. Outside the plate-glass windows, two highways loop around each other in the air carrying a steady stream of transport trucks through a blue sky. A remixed reggae song is humming through the speakers. Two wet eyebrows raised up into a high forehead. One foot then the other on the mint ice-cream coloured plank, two skinny elbows jerking in time to the music. 9 a.m. summer light splashing all over his wet curls and the surface of the pool. Two shoulders swinging, head bobbing along the length of the board. Then a graceful flop into the air between beats.

THE BOTTOM

Did you hear me? Did you have your eyes open?

Sit on the bottom, scream hello, take three sips of tea and one bite of cookie.

LIFEGUARD

The teenage lifeguard with the long slick ponytail and the booty shorts and a wad of gum is the high priestess of Adult Lane Swim. She drags the signs—Slow, Average, Average, Fast—into place at the head of each lane. She unreels the giant strings of prayer beads that divide the pool. She preaches a sermon through the voice of the radio DJ on whichever station she chooses to fill the echoey room with that morning. She sits with one leg draped over the aluminum handrail of her tall chair, a flip-flop swaying back and forth on the joint of her big toe. A skilled swimmer resigned to watching those less capable hobbling up and down the lanes gracelessly. She does two-hour shifts three times a week and she has trained herself not to look at the clock every five minutes. She has learned how to reach a meditative state beyond boredom in those two hours.

But at Free Swim (when the three water slides, two diving boards, and the Tarzan rope are open) she is more policewoman than guardian angel. No running on the pool deck, we don't hold our friends' heads underwater, it's very dangerous, you can't make out here, okay? I don't want to have to ask you to leave. She has never performed CPR on a baby before but she believes she would feel confident placing two fingers on a baby's damp chest and breathing it back to life.

DREAMS

I never dream I'm flying, I dream I'm swimming through the sky.

DRESSING ROOMS

A public place filled with naked bodies. This is where you learn what's in store for you. New mothers easing drumstick thighs into tiny swimsuits, hooking straps over delicate shoulders, shimmying trunks up to meet pinprick belly buttons. Old women whose skin hangs off them like a sloppy suit. So old their knees and elbows won't unbend, their skin is grey and puckered except where it's coloured by purple veins. A woman sitting on a bench by the playpen, holding a baby's head against her breast. A toddler in striped leggings but no shirt hops on one foot in front of her holding a sock above his head. Her breasts look heavy and her shoulders are curling in towards her sternum. You are proud of the new, masculine muscles growing beneath your breasts.

LEARNING LATE

A man stands in the shallow end, bent at the waist, rolling one heavy arm after the other into the water. A big man, baby stepping through the shallow end. His arms cycling up and out and over and under, again and again. He submerges his face and turns his head from side to side, a breath on the left and a breath on the right, feet inching along the tiled bottom.

Later I meet him on a narrow ledge in the deep end of the slow lane. His arms are stretched wide on either side, hands gripping the gutter, chest leaning out into the lane, panting.

"I just learned to swim last week, I'm sorry if I'm slowing you down." As he's letting go of the wall. I watch him plow down the lane, doing the dance he was rehearsing in the shallow end.

He has to muster a blind faith that he can dance his way across the deep end to a place where he can touch down.

I glide by him going in the opposite direction. Through my scratched goggles I see his face whip from side to side, not looking at the bottom of the pool dropping away beneath him.

ESCAPING THE INESCAPABLE

In a realm with less gravity you ache less. She has been ordered to wear inflatable arm cuffs and tread water. Wheeling her walker across the parking lot in February, getting the swimsuit on, summoning the breath to inflate the arm cuffs, easing backwards down the ladder into the pool at the speed an icicle freezes, all that is worth escaping the tug of the world on your joints for twenty minutes to a half hour.

THE MUSE CENTRE, ST. JOHN'S

When I was seven my dad used to take me swimming on weeknights. We played a game where I held on to his shoulders and he sank beneath the surface and started swimming towards the bottom of the deep end. Faster and deeper than I could ever swim on my own. I held on for as long as my tiny lungs would let me, afraid of going deeper and afraid of letting go. When the pressure on my lungs was too much I flapped my arms and kicked viciously til my head broke the surface. Treading water in the deep end I could see my dad's wobbly form far below me.

After the swim I would shuffle out of the women's dressing room in my salt-stained boots and puffy coat. Moving through the real world is heavy and slow and nothing like flying. We each got a tinfoil-wrapped chocolate-covered mint from the candy machine in the lobby before heading out into the winter night.

DES BISCUITS

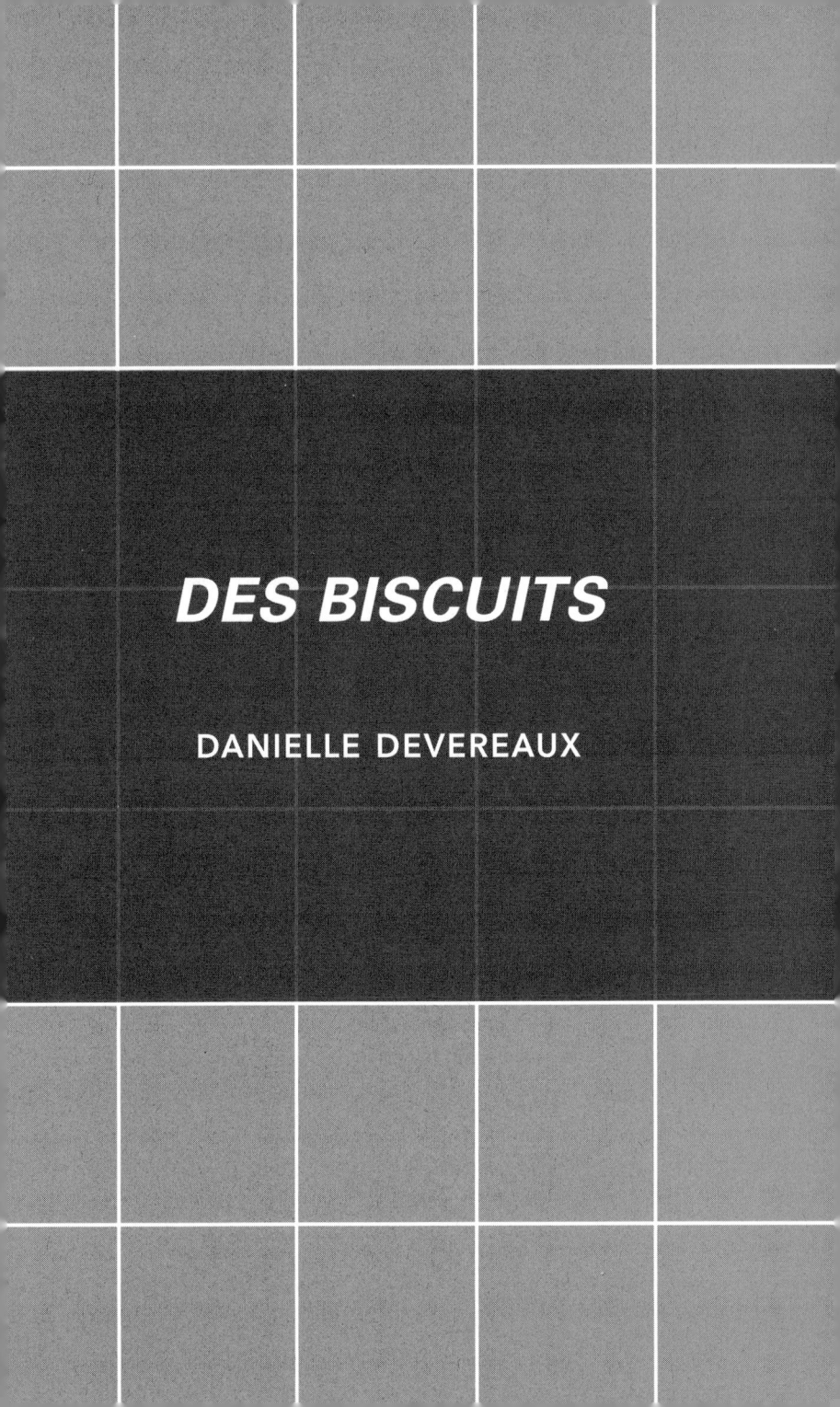

DANIELLE DEVEREAUX

I decided to give up cookies the year I was studying French in Quebec. It was a New Year's resolution. A person can eat quite a few cookies while studying and I'd decided, having taken note of both my grocery bill and the fit of my jeans, I was eating too many.

I liked studying French. I wasn't very good at it at first, but I was getting better, especially since the start of the new year, when I'd moved into an apartment with two Quebecois sisters. (They were twins—we'd joke that I was *la troisième jumelle*.) We spoke only French at home, so between my classes at L'Université Laval and *mes soeurs québécoises*, I'd gotten pretty good.

January, February, and most of March went fine, but one day in the middle of March my brain broke, or perhaps more accurately, was temporarily full to capacity. It was as though my mind needed a break to let all the French I'd learned so far sink a little deeper before it could let any more in. But it felt like I was back at the beginning; I had no idea how long the break would last or if the French I'd learned so far was gone for good. I was normally pretty chatty in class, but on this day I didn't say a word, nor did I understand a word out of *Madame's* mouth. It was as if I'd never heard a word of French before in my life. I was frustrated and grumpy and I needed a cookie.

After class I stopped at the grocery store to buy a bag of cookies before getting the bus back to my apartment. Standing in the cookie aisle I felt dejected, not only was my brain broken, I also couldn't keep a New Year's resolution. As punishment I did not let myself buy my favorite cookies—Mr. Christie soft-baked chocolate chip or a generic brand of vanilla creams—but instead bought Fig Newtons, because, as claimed in a Nabisco commercial going around at the time, the Fig Newton was not actually a cookie, but fruit and cake.

My bus ride home was forty-five minutes long. It was a gray March day. About ten minutes into the ride a woman and a little girl got on the bus. A man moved toward the front to meet them. They all looked happy to see one another. The adults kissed on both cheeks. The man took the little girl by the hand and found a couple of seats. The woman turned and walked

DES BISCUITS

back towards the front of the bus. When the child looked up and realized the woman was getting off the bus she started to scream, "*Maman! Maman!*" *Maman* turned, smiled, and with a wave stepped off the bus. The child howled.

I saw all this so clearly because I was sitting at the front of the bus, in the section where the seats line the sides and face the centre aisle. The man and the little girl sat in the first row of paired seats, facing the front of the bus, so we were sitting perpendicular to one another.

She howled through to the next stop and the next. The man tried to comfort the screaming child. He looked stricken. The bus was full, not overcrowded, but all the seats were taken. The other riders looked uncomfortable. It seemed she might howl the whole ride. When I reached into my backpack, pulled out the package of Fig Newtons and started to open them, the whole front of the bus sighed, "*Ah, des biscuits!*" Or maybe it was just the one older gentleman across from me who said that, but I could tell the others were thinking the same thing.

I turned to the child with the package of open cookies and said "*Biscuit?*" She stopped crying, scowled at me, took a cookie and dropped it. So I held the package out again. She took one and ate it. The man next to her looked happy enough to cry. "*Merci,*" he said, and then kept talking. He was probably explaining the situation, why he and the girl's mother had exchanged a child on a bus. Probably he was the kid's dad. Probably they were separated and he had his kid on the weekend and the child was finding it tough. Maybe he was saying that Fig Newtons were the girl's favourite and wasn't it funny that we had the same taste in cookies. Who knows? I don't know. All I understood was "*merci*" and that the child had stopped crying, so I just nodded, smiled, and offered her another cookie. Then I went home and had tea and a few cookies myself.

Eventually my French brain came back. And I quit the cookie ban.

Like a lot of women I've done my fair share of dieting and I've read quite a few articles about the perils of emotional eating. I know you shouldn't offer a kid a cookie every time she cries. I understand that, most times, when you're sad and frustrated and things aren't going your way, cookies are not the answer. But there are times, sometimes, when we could all use *un biscuit*.

PLEASURE AND OTHER NUTRITIOUS MATTERS

ELENA SLAWINSKA

Wednesday, October 14, 2015.
One o'clock.
Temperature +23°C.
Atmospheric pressure 1,018 mbar.
Wind SW 21 km/h *Libeccio*.

The Mediterranean Sea is calm and turquoise.

The beach is downwind and far enough not to carry the voices of the vacationers, in this season mostly Germans.

Not an unusual autumn day in Liguria.

The south-westerly wind from Libya seems to blow Gianni to our table as soon as we sit down. With his usual warmth, he hugs and kisses both Michael and me, updates us on his new granddaughter. Seeing that we are hungry, he gets to the point.

'I have fresh *acciughe* today, caught last night just around the point. Marinated or breaded and fried. I'd go raw, if I were you: they're almost alive.'

Nothing compares to marinated fresh anchovies: the intensity of olive oil, and the acidity of lemon and vinegar wed the tenderness of the raw fish in a grand feast. Gianni uses a touch of hot pepper, which brings the fish to swim in your mouth. Then, what it does to you, just as Gustave Flaubert describes in his mirage of lemon ice during a trip across the desert,

> *it bathes the uvula, glides over the tonsils, descends into the gullet, which is only too happy, and it falls into the stomach which bursts with laughing, so delighted it is.*

'Marinated!' we blurt out in unison.

One of his waiters has just brought a carafe of sparkling white wine.

'This one is on the house,' Gianni decrees.

Italy provides the ultimate food-based therapy to help us reconcile with life. We indulge in two long epicurean meals a day, often with friends or family. Social life revolves around mealtimes. You are always allowed and even encouraged to stretch your meals for hours. Yet, there is no flexibility for the starting time: fixed and confined to a one-hour slot. It does not surprise me to find an Internet entry for the proper time for lunch: *ora di pranzo*, which translates not as *time* but *hour* of lunch: 12:30 PM, slightly earlier in the north and later in the south but always punctual. No chance to find a restaurant open at 4 PM in Italy, even on Sunday.

There is a major distinction between the dictionary entries in Italian and English for *pranzo* and lunch. They have in common the meaning of representing a meal taken in the middle of the day, but, while in English lunch is often defined as a light meal, in Italian *pranzo* is the main meal of the day. Other meanings highlight its conviviality, richness, and abundance, such as in *pranzo di nozze* (you would always say *pranzo* even if the wedding celebration happens at night). One of the most interesting connotations of *pranzo* is that of space. Italian houses have a *sala da pranzo*, not a dining room, which is congruous with the importance of this meal in the culture.

Luckily, living in the United States and then in Canada has inoculated me against the bondage of meals at specific, fixed times and places. My new habit is declassed by my father as feeding, *nutrirsi*, as opposed to eating, *mangiare*. You should read the word *feeding* with a tone of contempt. Solitary ingestion of calories is a deadly sin to any Italian, as every day, twice a day, you are to infuse your food consumption with social rituals pivoting on conviviality. The ceremony includes admiration of the food, comparing it to previous similar recipes, assessing of someone's mother's inevitable superiority in the rendering of the recipe. A long, winding chat to accompany the many-course meal, all courses to be consumed separately, in a specific and immutable order, each on a clean new plate, every day, twice. Unthinkable on the other side of the Atlantic, where breakfast often slides into the middle of the day, and supper is so early to encroach on lunch. The one-course dish never contains a single food type but an odd assortment of colourful and, mostly incompatible, "things." I am sure you can hear the voice of my father here.

After the piscatorial introduction to our *pranzo*, Gianni is back for the main courses, *primo* and *secondo*.

'As a first course, try *spaghetti con porcini*,' he offers. 'I found them this morning in the woods up there, firm and big, twenty-five of them! All that rain in September, and then this heat…'

I look at Michael and we both nod at Gianni, mouths already watering with anticipation. Gianni always delivers. We rarely look at the restaurant's menu, daily hand-drawn with chalk on a school blackboard, standing by the entrance. Gianni anticipates our desires and has always the perfect suggestion.

'Red or white sauce?' asks the owner.

'White for me.'

'I get what she gets,' adds Michael. He knows I favour mushroom sauce without tomato: its acidity corrodes the fragile taste of the porcini.

'Good choice,' smiles Gianni and yells to his wife in the kitchen, '*Due porcini bianchi!*'

PLEASURE AND OTHER NUTRITIOUS MATTERS

In Italy, acidity is an adjective used to define unwanted qualities in food and in people. It is very difficult to pair wine with a dish based on tomato sauce. Have you noticed how it is common to order pizza with a beer but not with a glass of wine? The tannin of red wine and that of tomato add up to an unpleasant astringent sensation in the mouth. Acidity is a desirable quality in white wine, as it is responsible for vivacity and freshness of flavour but does not couple well with acidic food, like tomatoes. Acidity is also what you usually get in your *suocera*, your mother-in-law. Typically, the Italian mother-in-law interferes daily in the life of the married couple to "protect" her boy from the bad cooking of the new inexperienced wife. In the country of *mammoni*—adult men who never stop being mother-dependent—centuries of frustrated wives have coined the expression "acidic like a mother-in-law." To further make the point, there is a brand of sour cream in Italy that celebrates this coupling with its thirty-percent-fat "Panna Suocera." Sometimes, your *suocera* can also be highly tannic, like a sharp red wine that dries your palate on the first sip.

Gianni is back. The porcini are nutty, firm, and vaguely tasting of chestnuts, bonfires, and wet leaves. The sauce coats the spaghetti perfectly. Not too liquid, not too dense. Gianni holds a small grater in his left hand and an ugly-looking tuber in his right.

'Fancy some *tartufo?*'

The mix between a potato and a ginger root is the epitome of hypogean fungi. Its aroma is an array of simple perceptions with variable amplitude and intensity: garlic, hay, honey, spices, wet soil, ripe cheese. Matthew Frank calls idnology—the science dedicated to studying truffles—the tastiest of all "ologies."

Truffle enhances almost anything it is added to. Distinctly, the mood of the eater. Pliny the Elder defined it as a "miracle of nature," a "jewel of the ground"; Juvenal called it "son of the lightning."

A modicum of grated truffle rests on top of my pasta. An Elysian whiff intoxicates my nostrils.

"Food-ology" sometimes can be an Italian obsession. If you Google the sentence "eating or nourishing," you will not find much of an online discussion. But if you are Italian, you have at your disposal 213,000 results to the existential question "*mangiare o nutrirsi*," answered by philosophers, sociologists, psychologists, nutritionists, physicians, personal trainers, priests, chefs, and grandmas.

When my mother started to work as a young girl, she would come home for lunch—as all Italians do. Her mother was exasperated by her eating quickly out of the fridge and rushing out. 'Only to catch fleas and to study you don't need company!' *Mangiare da soli*? Impossible, and socially repulsive.

No chance to argue with grandma about that. Sitting, conversing, and dawdling *a tavola* is the way Italians grew up, where meals are defined by the shared pleasures of the table rather than by nutrition and caloric intake.

Gianni is asking if we want *secondo*, our next main course. *Agnello con carciofi*, his suggestion.

'Lamb and artichokes in this season? Isn't it an Easter dish?' I inquire with suspicion.

'Yes, we started to offer it all year around. You know, the tourists…'

'Are they fresh?' queries Michael.

'*Andiamo*! Nothing but fresh here! *No*?' Gianni's Sicilian pride punctuates the words by bringing together all the fingers of his right hand at their tips and menacingly waving the weapon close to Michael's nose.

Aren't we indulging too much in the lustful idolisation of food, of its rituals? Back in the North American continent, I feel liberated from the constraints of the Meal Law. I take a vacation from the ritualization of the act of eating, from its required conviviality, its stiff rules, its disciplinarians.

Take brunch. To my father, a sacrilege instigating a subversion of the meal ritual. To me, ominous in sound but a wicked idea. In the North American consumerist democracy, brunch relativizes time by extending breakfast into lunch, with a stretching and a multiplication of the hours involved. It pulverises classical cuisine and its segregation and sequencing of appetiser, main course, side dish, and dessert. The emphasis on spontaneous expression over the perfection of the formal meal feels like a liberation for the artist locked inside me. I agree with the Italian painter Marco Tirelli in defining brunch as the extreme amplification of the de-structured meal. Brunch does to gastronomy what the abstract expressionism of Jackson Pollock did to modern art. Brunch abates the distances of the full-course meal, which in my Italian family has taken a fixed form. Spatially, with my father sitting at the head of the table, a *capotavola*; Temporally, at immutable times, 12:30 PM and 8:30 PM; Sequentially, with a permanent order of courses, from *antipasto*, to *primo*, to *secondo*, to *dolce*.

'*Dolce?*'

How can we resist dessert? Even after three courses, I know that Gianni's tiramisu has few equals. Hints of java, a prelude to the much-needed coffee at the end of this long meal. It literally "pulls you up." Its name, ironically chosen by its creator, Roberto Linguanotto—a pastry chef in Treviso—was inspired by the fortifying sweets consumed in bordellos. Sinful pleasure has historically been associated with meals and, unfortunately, not only with aphrodisiac foods. It started with the Greek philosophers, repressing hedonistic joys by an excess of rationality.

PLEASURE AND OTHER NUTRITIOUS MATTERS

They were telling us to lead a virtuous life by abstaining from immediate physical pleasures. Temperance being one of the four cardinal virtues.

The contemporary Breatharians (who must be the extreme reincarnation of the Stoics in the way they deny themselves the joys of food) do not pollute their bodies and souls with the vulgarity of a chuck of beef, nor with the levity of lettuce. They nourish themselves by inhaling cosmic particles, the *prana* of the universe.

More moderate philosophies, such as the Slow Food Movement, propose "the vaccine of an adequate portion of sensual gourmandise pleasures, to be taken with slow and prolonged enjoyment" to counteract the hectic, fast-paced character of modern life. Since our existence cannot be described as chaotic or stressful, Michael and I enjoy more than adequate portions of voluptuous gratification from food and life by consuming them briskly and vigorously, in the moment, breathing through the nose. Tiramisu is the essence of kinetic pleasure, a dynamic carnal delight. It comes immediately, following Gianni's waving gesture at one of the waiters.

'Carpe Diem!' Michael dares me with a grin, before we bury our heads into the dessert in our intimate culinary race.

Like the best disciples of Aristippus of Cyrene, we let ourselves go to the physical ecstasy of this languorous *dolce vita*. The gossamer weight of the Mascarpone cream sits delicately on the *Savoiardi* base, kissed by unsweetened espresso and topped by a teeny explosion of dark cocoa.

Caffè comes when we are back from heaven.

Gianni knows how we drink *caffè*.

Ristretto, a "shortened" espresso, after all else is finished. Black, one sugar for me, none for Michael.

Espresso, the only form of coffee it is acceptable to order if you are Italian (or if you accompany one), is not meant to coexist with food. You do not order *caffè* together with dessert, let alone with your pasta. It comes only when the table has been cleared of plates and bread. Some restaurants make a point of removing salt and pepper before bringing coffee. This rule is so strict that, if you order a *caffè* before finishing your meal, you are immediately labelled by everyone in the restaurant as a hopeless barbarian outsider. Besides the draconian table etiquette, the rationale behind this is that an espresso is too small to keep warm while you are eating *dolce*. Unless you eat tiramisu like Michael and me.

It is said in Italy that you should be cursing while drinking your *caffè*, which is to be served at the temperature of molten lead. In one sip (easy, given the quantity) and, if you are at the bar, standing at the counter (again a by-product of its size) and paying cash. *Caffè* is cheap and, at the bar, it is generally ordered alone.

PLEASURE AND OTHER NUTRITIOUS MATTERS

But we are sitting at the restaurant, and I maintain that I need to taste coffee, not be injured by it. I let it cool. Then, in one sip, surprising for such a quick motion, I can have an intense taste experience of coffee. Its nutty volatile aroma drifts up to the nostrils. Its full heavy body, perceived when the tongue pushes against the palate. Its minimal bitterness in the back of the mouth, the sweetness on the tip of the tongue. Trained oral papillae can conjure a rich tactile experience.

While I luxuriate in my coffee tasting, I remember that, according to the Merlo Coffee barista—who won the biannual "Australia's Favourite Coffee" twice in a row in 2012 and 2014— he or she who orders *ristretto* must be a Purist's Pour, a staunch perfectionist with unreasonably high standards. Controlling and likely a politician. I have never had a Merlo *ristretto*, but I suspect I may not like it.

In Italy instead, I am always told that, although restrained as I am in ordering a ristretto, I "poison it" with sugar. As maintained by the Australian barista's pairing of personality and coffee choice, serious and committed characters always order some variation of black coffee, no milk or sugar frills. "If you need sugar in your coffee, perhaps you don't actually like coffee," patronizes an American website, managed by a coffee-expert, someone that, no doubt, has attended Barista Camps, US Coffee Championships and all sorts of professional development activities to raise his consciousness about coffee. I wonder what he thinks of the numerous cappuccino drinkers among his compatriots.

For me, *caffè* is just one of the various pleasures in life. In a perfectionist manner, I demand high-quality coffee and I allow the sugar to raise only my blood glucose but not my sense of guilt.

Ammazzacaffè is being served, again courtesy of Gianni. Grappa for Michael, *Limoncello* for me.

I am not sure why it is called "coffee killer." Was the taste of coffee so poor in the past that it needed obliteration? Coffee sommeliers appreciate a moderate lingering *retrogusto* as one of the elements of quality of the coffee. The aftertaste must remain in the mouth for a little while to exalt, transform, and enrich the sensations of drinking coffee. Why does a digestive liquor have to kill it?

Lunch is sleepily coming to an end.

No, don't go there! Doggy bag is a taboo. For sixty-five years Americans have practiced the art of taking home scraps of food. Finally, last August, there was a serious poll in Italy asking, "Are you favourable to the doggy bag?" The answers were:

20% Yes, I paid and food should not be wasted.
25% No, it is an inelegant practice.
55% Yes, but I am ashamed to ask.

PLEASURE AND OTHER NUTRITIOUS MATTERS

The Mediterranean's ancestral frame of mind is chiefly concerned with what others think and how to look good in their eyes. Hope of changing this—besides the above 20%—include a recent court sentence in favour of a client who wanted to bring home his leftovers and was prevented from doing so by the owner of a restaurant in Trento because "It does not look good." But the most impressive and truly Italian move toward accepting this custom with long historic roots even in Italy—it was started by the Romans and then dropped during the Middle Ages—is the designer doggy bag: one architect, four designers, and three illustrators got together and created small branded plastic containers appealing to the Italian's complete submission to fashion and design. They were exhibited in a national art venue and are now in restaurants. In light of the designer doggy bag, an answer can be added to the previous questionnaire, which will reshuffle the percentages:

75% Yes, but only with style.

Wednesday, October 14, 2015.
Four o'clock.
Temperature +22°C.
Atmospheric pressure 1,031 mbar.
Wind SE 15 km/h *Scirocco*.

The sea is flat as a table, of a hypnotic blue.
High-pitched coloratura of elder Italians has replaced the

barking gutturals of the German tourists on the beach.

A pleasurable autumn day in Liguria, where we follow a dietary model characterized by abundant fresh pleasure, conviviality as a source of healthy fats, and negligible amounts of remorse for high-calorie intake and caffeine consumption.

We follow a diet listed by UNESCO in the World Intangible Heritage List as a "Cultural Practice."

NIGHT WALK

AMY DONOVAN

*T*exture. The forest has texture. You can feel it whispering in the air. The sense of space when the pines open onto beeches or when the forest opens to the lake. The solidity of the moss wall on your left, the increase in vertical space when the slope on your right becomes steeper. You breathe sweet night air. The scent of balsam hovers on your nostrils. It lingers on every hair in your nose.

You touch the moss. It is springy, damp, feathered, and furred. The nerve endings in your hand fire up, and for a second the sensitive skin on your fingertips seems porous. A tingle of something bigger than you slips in, deep.

All your senses pulse outward from the tingle. What are you missing the rest of the time? What might you be, if you were always this tuned in?

You draw in more forest air. You want to gulp as much as

possible.

Your eyes are wide open and all you can see is the deep, three-dimensional blackness of this moonless night in the boreal forest.

The last thing you remember really seeing were the bunchberry flowers, shaped like rounded-off stars. White flowers remain open at night, you heard, to attract moths. Unlike colourful blooms, which open only in sunlight, only for butterflies. You found yourself sympathizing with the moths. You imagined them as brown and bland, but then you remembered the luna moth. You blurted this out and then regretted breaking the silence.

The guide didn't mind. "Luna moths always emerge from their cocoons in the morning," she told you, "and at first their wings are soft and small. They fill them with fluids to enlarge them, and then they have to hide for two hours while their wings harden."

Two hours, you thought.

"It doesn't seem like a long time," she said, "but they never live for more than seven days. Most moths don't even eat as adults. They don't have mouths. They mate and die."

You prickled a little at this. Your mouth. Your limbs still, but coursing with energy.

"I hope the mating is good," said someone in the back of the group.

NIGHT WALK

"I doubt the moth knows the difference," his wife shot back. But you can't see why it wouldn't.

White flowers smell more strongly at night, too. You couldn't pinpoint the smell of the bunchberry flowers, but there was a sweetness that was not just trees. A better nose would be able to tell. You were left thinking this, at least, is a pleasure the moth must know.

Snakes, you learn, taste smell with their tongues. Catch scent particles, transfer information to the brain. Suddenly your tongue seems thick, cumbersome. You open your mouth, let your tongue reach out and taste the air. There is a tang of balsam, a flicker of the lake and everything in there that is alive and green and juicy.

Or maybe you are imagining it.

Some snakes can see heat. You wonder what this looks like. Then you wonder, humid summer air sliding along your skin, if your body is seeing it now, as your eyes see only darkness.

Later, the clouds will dissipate. Stars will blink into the sky. By now your night vision will be fully developed, pupils vast and receiving. You will wonder how you never noticed how many stars there are.

Against this sky, pines will make silhouettes that are like watercolour, like Japanese ink, like feathers drifting on a breeze. You will connect their slight waving to the whispering you

BEST KIND

have been hearing, and you will feel the thrill of fitting two perfect pieces together.

Later still, you will swim. You weren't prepared for this, no swimsuit, no towel. But the air has stayed thick with rare August heat. Your lungs wrench as your body is dizzied by the change in temperature. Your feet meet slimy eelgrass and you flail until you are on your back on the surface of the water, a starfish-shaped human staring up—and forgetting the cold, because now you know why, in pictures, the sky looks like a big sphere. The stars are not just in the sky but in the water, too, little bobbing lights surrounding you. You will soften into them. You'll become aware of how short your senses fall compared to how much there is to feel; then you'll soften out of that awareness, too. Surrounded by stars, you will breathe.

An owl call will cut in, clear and close. The "*hoo-hoo hoo-hoooo*" of the barred owl.

You'll remember what the guide, floating next to you, said about the toad: breathing through its skin. You'll wonder, is this what it feels like?

But that's later. For now, piercing darkness. And a sound that makes everything in you clench.

A howl.

Every cell spikes to high alert: *where is it?*

Then the howl becomes multiple, shapes itself into a chorus of yipping. You realize the coyotes are far away. They are talking

NIGHT WALK

to one another. Singing.

They are singing and the song is not about you.

Your shoulders loosen. The song is not about you but about the forest, and the forest is allowing you to hear it. You tilt your head upward.

The musculoskeletal structure of an owl's face is a slipway that sends sound into the ears.

You listen.

Hunting animals, you learned earlier, have poor colour vision because what they need to see is movement. A coyote doesn't care what colour prey is, only that it is small—small enough to be killed—and that it moves: alive enough to be eaten.

They see very well in the dark. Much better than you. Besides that their eyes have lots more rods—the cells that capture light—they have what's called the *tapetum lucidum*. It's a reflective membrane on the back of the retina that bounces visual information through the eye a second time, giving the animal a second chance to process what it is seeing. It's known as the mirror membrane; it's the reason animals' eyes glow in the dark.

You do a quick, furtive scan of the forest around you: no glowing pinpricks. Your disappointment takes you by surprise.

Then you hear another far-off yip, and you smile. You were never alone.

You pause in a place that is thickly forested, where white spruce and birch crowd together and make it dark again. You settle into this darkness. You feel enclosed and it's like your whole body can breathe better than it knew was possible. You are here and nowhere else. You don't know how to get anywhere else. You haven't checked your phone in hours.

You hear that you will soon be back in the world you know, of cars and fluorescent lights, beeping and buzzing. Something drops in you, but the guide is still talking. She is saying how little dark sky is left in the world; she is asking if maybe there is some part of human experience—of animal experience— we are losing by banishing darkness from our lives, she is—she is laughing, she is exclaiming: "Did you hear that?"

You did hear it: the tiniest of squeaks, a papery whoosh of movement. You thought nothing of it.

"A bat!" she says. You feel how she lights up. "We used to see them all the time but I've only encountered three this whole summer."

You hear that bats all over North America are dying from white-nose syndrome, which keeps them awake during winter, when they should be hibernating, when there are no insects for them to eat.

You imagine it: airborne, furred, but growing thinner. Wheeling around in blasting sunlight you are not used to, wondering why there is no food, why it is so cold, why you cannot sleep. You have no wings but you do have warm

NIGHT WALK

blood. You can imagine cold, can imagine hunger.

Dead bats, she is saying. Millions of them. Maybe ninety percent.

You feel a sharp wedge of sadness but something else overcoming it. Somewhere high up, a wind brushes through trembling aspen. The leaves rustle. They chat. A stand of aspen is not a group of individual trees but one big living organism, connected by an intricate root system. You think you can feel it down there somewhere, pulsing.

"Don't bats hide?" you ask, remembering something learned in childhood about dark and secret places. "Could there be colonies we don't know about?"

You can't see it, but you can feel her look toward you. This is proprioception: a sense you can't capture in words or even identify as you are making use of it, but that is in you all the time, keeping you from walking into walls. The body's gut knowledge of nearby physicality. Another thing you did not even know about, going about your lit-up diurnal life.

"Yes," she says. "There are colonies we don't know about. They are the hope. That one bat we just heard is the hope."

The guide likes your interest, your thoughtful questions. When everyone is leaving you ask: "Don't you get scared?"

"There's no reason to," she says. "But this hike never feels routine. There's always a little part of me that isn't quite sure we'll make it out again. It keeps me interested."

She laughs when you tense up. "It's perfectly safe. A coyote or bear would never approach a group this big."

You think of the coyotes but her eyes are sparkling. People are starting to turn headlights on and she says, "Close your eyes, your night vision!"

You squeeze your eyes shut, feel that little hit of shifting equilibrium even though you could hardly see a thing with eyes open.

The smooth rental vehicles pull away. "Let's swim," she says.

The lake holds you. Each breath makes wavelets that slip along the water's surface then disappear into the dark. Through your peripheral vision, where the lamentably inefficient rods in your own eyes congregate, you see the rounded silhouettes of mountains all around you; they hold you, too.

These mountains ripple from Newfoundland to Alabama. Three hundred million years ago they were ten kilometres tall.

You think of bits of them crumbling into the ocean. You imagine glaciers, whose sheer size and majesty you know you cannot imagine. Huge white beings moving along the landscape—slipping, you wonder, or roaring?—smoothing out the plateau, scooping up a chunk of earth and leaving behind the valley in which you are floating. Ten thousand years ago. An eternity and not long at all.

She talked about preserving darkness, and you think, now, how it's not just darkness. It's *this* darkness. The shape of it, its

NIGHT WALK

densities and topographies. The weight of its air, the taste of its scents, the tonal depths of its shadows. You wonder about other darknesses. You wonder how it is that all night you have hardly been able to see anything, and yet you have never felt so intensely that you are not in any dark place, but this one. And—this you'd never dare say out loud, this you know you will laugh at in the morning, in your cabin with its microwave and dusty floral sofa—you have never felt so intensely that *this* place knows you are here; that, in voices softer than whispers, in caresses that never touch, in smells smaller than a particle of air, this place has something to say. You have never tried so hard to hear.

There's a loud crash somewhere near the edge of the lake, followed by the splashing of something large. You both jump. Your legs tangle with the reaching arms of water plants but do not touch bottom. You pedal your feet until you are treading water; you calm your gasping lungs then look around. The splashing evens into rippling.

It takes a moment for your eyes to focus, and then you see it: a big black lump gliding through the water, more or less toward you, with such grace and ease that you don't believe your eyes when you see the silhouette of antlers.

"What a beauty," the guide breathes, and you are filled with something like warmth, something like magic, something like, maybe, gratitude. There is this lake, the water no longer cold, the stars above, the mountains around. There was the sound of water and now there is the sound of almost-silence. There are three mammals, floating. Held.

The moose passes just a couple of feet from you. If you reached out, you could touch him. You do not reach out. You do not even breathe.

He does not seem to register that he is not alone—although, you will realize later when you think about it, he probably never deludes himself that he is alone.

He carries on at his languid pace, more waltzing with the water than swimming through it. Eventually he disappears in the purple-black darkness. There is more splashing, then the distant crackle of branches. He has reached the other shore and moved on. Somewhere, a toad trills.

PAINTING THE CURLEW

MATTHEW HOLLETT

The eskimo curlew lives in a nest of cardboard and cotton, the size of a shoebox, and the collections manager wears cotton gloves when she picks it up to show us. The feathers on its belly have a distinct swirl that reminds me of the way wind rustles long grass. The curlew has no eyes, since the specimen was prepared in 1869. Nathalie, the Natural History Collections Manager, tells us that its skull is intact, but otherwise its bones have been replaced by cotton batting. The eskimo curlew is extinct.

I am visiting the curlew with Don McKay, who has asked me to design a small chapbook of poems. Before we walk over to The Rooms, I meet Don and he shows me a drawing of the curlew in a Chilean field guide. Eskimo curlews were once one of the most numerous shorebirds in the western Arctic, Don tells me. From their breeding grounds in the Yukon and Northwest

Territories, huge flocks migrated all the way to Argentina. Along the way, they'd stop in Labrador to gorge themselves on berries.

By the late 1800s, two million eskimo curlews were slaughtered per year. They were already in peril in 1833, when John James Audubon, celebrated ornithologist and painter, voyaged to what was then part of Labrador (now Quebec) in search of subjects for his grand project, *Birds of America*. Having recently suffered a stroke, Audubon was content to stay on board the vessel and draw, while his assistants went hunting for specimens. His *Labrador Journal* preserves his impressions from an eventful two months living along the Strait of Belle Isle. "The hold of the vessel has been floored, and our great table solidly fixed in a tolerably good light under the main hatch; it is my intention to draw whenever possible, and that will be many hours, for the daylight is with us nearly all the time in those latitudes, and the fishermen say you can do with little sleep, the air is so pure."

Officially, *Numenius borealis* is listed as critically endangered, not extinct. "Recovery is not considered feasible at this time," according to Environment Canada's 2007 *Recovery Strategy for the Eskimo Curlew*, "because no nests have been located in 140 years and there are very few, if any, individuals left in existence. We recommend that no recovery action be undertaken other than continued monitoring of reported sightings." The last confirmed sighting of an eskimo curlew was in September 1963, when a hunter shot one in Barbados. The last recorded sighting in Canada was at Battle Creek, Labrador, in 1932.

PAINTING THE CURLEW

"*The Curlews are coming*," writes Audubon, "is as much of a saying here as that about the Wild Pigeons in Kentucky. What species of Curlew, I know not yet, for none have been killed, but one of our men [...] assured me that he had seen some with bills about four inches long, and the body the size of a Wild Pigeon. The accounts given of these Curlews border on the miraculous, and I shall say nothing about them till I have tested the fishermen's stories."

How does a small parcel of feathers and muscle propel itself from the Northwest Territories to Argentina and back? This curlew has also travelled from Labrador to London, having been for a time in the archives of the British Museum, and now sleeps soundly in St. John's. Nathalie tells us about the natural history collection. "We get specimens donated, mostly," she says. "As you prepare a specimen, you lose parts of it that you can't get back—its weight, the colour of its eyes, the contents of its stomach. So you record those things as you go. For a bird, it's really just the skin you end up with, unless you preserve it in liquid, which is a very different process. We have hundreds of different species in the collection," she says, "but this is the only eskimo curlew."

Audubon was once mailed three dead eskimo curlew by an admirer from Ipswich, Massachusetts. It wasn't until he travelled north that he saw them, briefly, alive. "This afternoon we all went ashore, through a high and frightful sea which drenched us to the skin, and went to the table-lands; there we found the true Esquimau Curlew, *Numenius borealis* […] I have seen many hundreds this afternoon, and shot seven. They fly in compact bodies, with beautiful evolutions, overlooking a great extent of country ere they make choice of a spot on which to alight; this is done wherever a certain berry, called here *Curlew berry*, proves to be abundant. Here they balance themselves, call, whistle, and of common accord come to the ground, as the top of the country here must be called. They devour every berry, and if pursued squat in the manner of Partridges. A single shot starts the whole flock."

Empetrum nigrum, the crowberry, is sometimes still referred to as the curlew berry. "Their food consists almost entirely of the Crow-berry, which grows on all the hill-sides in astonishing profusion," writes Elliott Coues of the eskimo curlew, in his *Notes on the Ornithology of Labrador* (1861). "It is also called the 'Bear-berry' and 'Curlew-berry'… This is their principal and favourite food, and the whole intestine, the vent, legs, bill, throat, and even the plumage are more or less stained with the deep purple juice."

At The Rooms, the curlew's feet are tied with an identification card containing its Latin name in impossibly precise calligraphy: *Numenius borealis*. *Numenius* comes from *Noumenios* or *new moon*, because the curlew's beak is a sliver of crescent moon. There is a crack in its beak. When Nathalie lifts its body out of the box, it leaves a curlew-shaped impression in the cotton. I expect the body to be floppy, but it is very stiff. Held aloft in white gloves, it's hard to believe it was ever alive. It feels as if it fell to earth from elsewhere, like a meteor, as if the patterns on its chest are from where it caught fire in the atmosphere.

"They are frequently so fat," writes George H. Mackay in *Habits of the Eskimo Curlew* (1892), "that when they strike the ground after being shot their skin bursts, exposing a much thicker layer of fat than is usually seen in other birds, hence their local name *Doughbird*, from the saying 'as fat as dough.' They are considered by epicures the finest eating of any of our birds, and consequently they are watched for and sought after by sportsmen with great perseverance."

The curlew lies in its nest. It looks warm, or as if it wants to be warm. I imagine curling up with the curlew in its cotton bed, pulling the cardboard lid over us, and lying there in the archives until someone comes looking.

Once in a while someone does come looking. Nathalie shows us a photocopy of a painting by Helen Gregory, who several years ago made a series of studies of specimens in the natural history collection: a splayed crow with its eyes closed, four blue tanagers hanging by their feet, a giant squid's tangled tentacles. She exhibited them at The Rooms in a show called *Unrequited*

Death. Helen painted the eskimo curlew framed by its cardboard box, the same distinct swirl of feathers on its chest. "I really loved Helen's exhibition," Nathalie says. "After here it was shown in Ottawa, and I always wonder what happened to that painting of the curlew. I suppose it's in some collection now."

"I have been drawing at the *Numenius borealis*; I find them difficult birds to represent," writes Audubon. His watercolour of the "Esquimau Curlew" is prescient: a female sprawls lifeless on the mossy ground, while a male bird bends its neck towards the earth. "The young men went on shore and brought me four more; every one of the lads observed to-day the great tendency these birds have, in squatting to elude the eye, to turn the tail towards their pursuer, and to lay the head flat."

George Mackay, too, describes the elusive habits of the curlew: "They fly low after landing, sweeping slowly over the ground, apparently looking it over, generally standing motionless for quite a little while after alighting, which, owing to their general color approximating so closely to withered grass, renders it difficult at times to perceive them. I have had a flock of fifty or sixty alight within thirty yards of me, and have been unable to make out more than two or three birds."

A hundred years earlier, in his *Journal of Transactions and Events during a Residence of nearly Sixteen Years on the Coast of Labrador*, George Cartwright wrote, "To shoot Curlews, or grey or golden Plover: Preserve one or two of the birds, or stuff their skins in a standing posture, and fix a bit of strong wire to their legs, to fix them in the ground by. Dig a hole in the ground which is frequented by them [...] with a hole left on one side to get into it, and a small one in front to shoot through; the preserved birds must be pricked into the ground at a proper distance from the hut; an assistant must walk round to drive the birds towards the hut, & the shooter whistle to them in their own natural note, which will bring them to him."

Nathalie holds up the curlew and I shoot it with my DSLR.

BEST KIND

A few months after visiting The Rooms, I paint the curlew. Looking at my photograph, I trace the shape of the curlew on a small piece of watercolour paper with a pencil. Its body holds the memory of a shoreline. I draw the wriggled curve of its neck, the way its wings widen the sides of its body like eyelids. The darkness of its feet, coming to a slick point like a brush dipped in ink.

I paint the curlew's cotton bed with a cat's-tongue brush, with water and a speck of burnt umber, making a yellow so light I can't see the paint until it dries. Its beak is black and stiff as a candle wick, and I paint it with burnt umber and indigo, without water. Its feathers still hold the colour of reeds and rushes, and its chest is patterned with marks like the footprints of birds in sand. Ripples run through its feathers like light dappling water. Where its feathers run white I leave the paper bare.

When I arrive home on the day we visit The Rooms, I wonder if I can find an image of Helen Gregory's curlew painting. So I search online, and am astonished to find not just an image, but the painting itself. It's listed for sale in a local classified ad: *Large acrylic on canvas painting of an Eskimo Curlew specimen in a museum drawer. Artist: Helen Gregory. 2009. 30" wide × 6 ft high. Price: $9,500.*

In the photos on Kijiji you can see the painting hanging in someone's house in St. John's. It's much larger than I'd imagined—it hangs beside a door, and the curlew's cardboard box is almost as tall as the door. The painting looks like an adjacent door, a door to elsewhere, the curlew's cotton nest as beguiling as a warm bed. It's just the right size for curling up inside.

CLIVE WEARING WRITES

(AND WRITES AND WRITES)

HIS AUTOBIOGRAPHY

JOAN SULLIVAN

CHAPTER / SCENE I

Clive Wearing writes:

7:46 a.m.: I wake for the first time.[1]

Journalist. Is it possible to define autobiography? ...The definition of autobiography might be: 'a retrospective prose narrative produced by a real person concerning his own existence, focusing on his individual life, in particular on the developments of his personality.'[2]

Deborah Wearing. It was as if every waking moment was the

---

[1] Louise France, "The Death of Yesterday," *The Observer*, January, 23, 2005, http://www.guardian.co.uk/books/2005/jan/23/biography.features3/print.

[2] Philippe Lejeune, "The Autobiographical Contract," in *French Literary Theory Today: A Reader*, ed. Tzvetan Todorov (Cambridge: Cambridge University Press, 1982), 192-3.

first waking moment. Clive was under the constant impression that he had just emerged from unconsciousness because he had no evidence in his own mind of ever being awake before… "I haven't heard anything, seen anything, touched anything, smelled anything," he would say. "It's like being dead."[3]

Clive Wearing crosses the first line out. He writes:

7:47 a.m.: This illness has been like death till NOW. All senses work.[4]

Dr. Oliver Sacks. Though one cannot have direct knowledge of one's own amnesia, there may be ways to infer it: from the expression on people's faces when one has repeated something half a dozen times; when one looks down at one's coffee cup and finds that it is empty; when one looks at one's diary and sees entries in one's own handwriting. Lacking memory, lacking direct experiential knowledge, amnesiacs have to make hypotheses and inferences, and they usually make plausible ones. They can infer that they have been doing *something*, been *somewhere*, even though they cannot recollect what or where. Yet Clive, rather than making plausible guesses, always came to the conclusion that he had just been "awakened," that he had been "dead."[5]

---

[3] Oliver Sacks, "The Abyss," *The New Yorker*, September 24, 2007, http://www.newyorker.com/reporting/2007/09/24/070924fa_fact_sacks?printable=true

[4] France.

[5] Sacks.

CLIVE WEARING WRITES

Clive Wearing crosses the second line out. He writes:

8:07 a.m.: I AM awake.[6]

Journalist. The 'identity' of the narrator and the protagonist which autobiography implies is most often marked by the first person.[7]

CHAPTER / SCENE II

Clive Wearing. Are you the Prime Minister?[8]

Journalist. Imagine that I right now took out your memory. What would be left? Nothing.[9] Memory really defines who we are.[10]

Clive Wearing. Are you the Queen of England?[11] Are you from the U. N.?[12]

Sacks. Just the U.S.[13]

Deborah Wearing. This is Dr. Sacks.[14]

---

[6] France.
[7] Lejeune, 194.
[8] France.
[9] Tony Buzan qtd. in *Where Did I Put My Memory?* Documentary. Written and directed by Josh Freed. (2010: Morag Loves Forget It Inc. and Forget It Productions Inc.), https://www.youtube.com/watch?v=lMEVYHIB33I
[10] Gary Small qtd. in *Where Did I Put My Memory?*
[11] France.
[12] Sacks.
[13] Ibid.
[14] Ibid.

Clive Wearing. Been to Buckingham Palace?[15]

Sacks. Clive had no idea who I was, little idea who anyone was, but this bonhomie allowed him to make contact, to keep a conversation going.[16]

Deborah Wearing. It's because they are the first person he has seen since waking from 'unconsciousness' that minute, so they must, he presumes, be important.[17]

Clive Wearing. Your Highness.[18]

Journalist. He was forty-six years old. His wife was twenty-seven. They had been married barely six months. It began with a headache…[19]

Sacks. He was struck by a brain infection—a herpes encephalitis—affecting especially the parts of his brain concerned with memory. He was left with a span of only seconds.[20]

Deborah Wearing. His ability to perceive what he saw and heard was unimpaired. But he did not seem to be able to retain anything for more than a blink. Indeed, if he did blink, his

---

[15] Ibid.
[16] Ibid.
[17] France.
[18] Sacks.
[19] France.
[20] Sacks.

eyelids parted to reveal a new scene. The view before the blink was utterly forgotten. Each blink, each glance away and back, brought him an entirely new view. I tried to imagine how it was for him…Something akin to a film with bad continuity, the glass half empty, then full, the cigarette suddenly longer, the actor's hair now tousled, now smooth. But this was real life, a room changing in ways that were physically impossible.[21]

Journalist. What did you do yesterday? To answer this question you employ your *autobiographical memory*. Our autobiographical memory is our record of daily experience…part of our sense of identity as beings with a determinate past…our catalogue of specific episodes in which we interacted with significant people.[22]

Sacks. Clive no longer has any inner narrative.[23]

CHAPTER / SCENE III

Clive Wearing writes:

8:31 a.m.: Now I am really, completely awake.[24]

---

[21] Deborah Wearing qtd. in Sacks, "The Abyss."

[22] William Hirstein, Brain Fiction (Cambridge, Massachusetts: MIT Press, 2005), 43.

[23] Sacks.

[24] Gary Marcus, "The Woman Who Can't Forget and the Man Who Can't Remember," Wired Magazine 17:04, http://www.wired.com/print/medtech/health/magazine/17-04/ff_perfectmemory.

Deborah Wearing. He's not keeping a diary.[25]

Journalist. In a way all writers are obsessed with recollection.[26]

Sacks. Deborah wrote of how, coming in one day, she saw him "holding something in the palm of one hand, and repeatedly covering and uncovering it with the other hand as if he were a magician practising a disappearing trick. He was holding a chocolate. He could feel the chocolate unmoving in his left palm, and yet every time he lifted his hand he told me it revealed a brand new chocolate.

"Look!" he said. "It's new!"

"It's the same chocolate," I said gently.

"No…look! It's changed. It wasn't like that before…Look! It's different again! How do they do it?"[27]

Clive Wearing crosses the first line out. He writes:

9:06 a.m.: Now I am perfectly, overwhelmingly awake.[28]

Sacks. This dreadful journal, almost void of any other content but these passionate assertions and denials, intending to affirm

---

[25] Deborah Wearing, *Life Without Memory: The Case of Clive Wearing*, Part 1b, https://www.youtube.com/watch?v=ymEn_YxZqZw.

[26] France.

[27] Sacks.

[28] Marcus.

CLIVE WEARING WRITES

existence and continuity but forever contradicting them, was filled anew each day, and soon mounted to hundreds of almost identical pages. It was a terrifying and poignant testament to Clive's mental state, his lostness, in the years that followed his amnesia...[29] [A] lost soul. Was it possible he had really been "de-souled" by the disease?[30]

Clive Wearing crosses the second line out. He writes:

9:34 a.m.: Now I am superlatively, actually awake.[31]

Sacks. Another profoundly amnesic patient I knew some years ago dealt with his abysses of amnesia by fluent confabulations. He was wholly immersed in his quick-fire inventions and had no insight into what was happening; so far as he was concerned, there was nothing the matter. He would confidently identify or misidentify me as a friend of his, a customer in his delicatessen, a kosher butcher, another doctor—as a dozen different people in the course of a few minutes. This sort of confabulation was not one of conscious fabrication. It was, rather, a strategy, a desperate attempt—unconscious and almost automatic—to provide a sort of continuity, a narrative continuity, when memory, and thus experience, was being snatched away every instant.[32]

---

[29] Sacks.
[30] Sacks, describing another amnesia patient, in France.
[31] Marcus.
[32] Sacks.

Journalist. The only times of feeling alive were when Deborah visited him.[33]

Clive Wearing. (*to Deborah Wearing, who is leaving*) I adore everything about you. I could kiss you all day.[34]

Deborah Wearing exits.

Journalist. But the moment she left, he was desperate again, and by the time she got home, ten or fifteen minutes later, she would find repeated messages from him on her answering machine.[35]

Clive Wearing. (*picking up the phone, dialing*) Please come and see me, darling—it's been ages since I've seen you. Please fly here at the speed of light.[36]

Sacks. He remembers almost nothing unless he is actually doing it; then it may come to him.[37]

Journalist. He knows his home phone number but has no memory of making calls.[38]

Clive Wearing. (*picking up the phone, dialing*) Hello, love, 'tis me, Clive. It's five minutes past four and I don't know what's going

---

[33] Ibid.
[34] France.
[35] Sacks.
[36] Ibid.
[37] France.
[38] Sacks.

on here. I'm awake for the first time and I haven't spoken to anyone…[39]

Journalist. No one knew how much of his brain had been affected.[40]

Clive Wearing. (*picking up the phone, dialing*) Darling? Hello, it's me, Clive. It's quarter past four and I'm awake now for the first time. It all just happened a minute ago, and I want to see you.[41]

Journalist. At first he was manically euphoric. He'd jump out of wardrobes, waltz down the ward, play the hospital jester. On the whole this jocularity protected people from registering what had happened to his mind.[42]

Clive Wearing. (*picking up the phone, dialing*) Darling? It's me, Clive, and it's eighteen minutes past four and I'm awake. My eyes have just come on about a minute ago. I haven't spoken to anyone yet.[43]

Journalist. Then his mood changed. He wept continuously for over a month. He became obsessed with finding out what had happened to him.[44]

---

[39] France.
[40] Ibid.
[41] Ibid.
[42] Ibid.
[43] Ibid.
[44] France.

BEST KIND

Sacks. A young psychologist saw Clive for a period of time in 1990 and kept a verbatim record of everything he said: "Can you imagine one night five years long? No dreaming, no waking, no touch, no taste, no smell, no sight, no sound, no hearing, nothing at all. It's like being dead."[45]

Journalist. For complex systems such as the brain, we may learn more about the functional relationships when they cease to function properly than when everything is working smoothly.[46]

Clive Wearing. (*picking up the phone, dialing*) I just want to speak to you.[47]

CHAPTER / SCENE IV

Sacks. I saw Clive's journal by the washstand—he has now filled up scores of volumes, and the current one is always kept in this exact location:[48]

"I am awake." "I am conscious." "2:20 p.m.: This time properly awake...2:14 p.m.: this time finally awake...2:35 p.m.: this time completely awake...At 9:40 p.m. I awoke for the first time, despite my previous claims...I was fully conscious at 10:35 p.m.,

---

[45] Sacks.
[46] Jonathan K. Foster, *Memory: A Very Short Introduction* (Oxford: Oxford University Press, 2009), 90.
[47] France.
[48] Sacks.

and awake for the first time in many, many weeks."[49]

Journalist. Autobiography is the literary genre which, by its very content, most clearly exhibits the confusion between the author and the individual person…it expresses the cry for existence of personal identity itself.[50]

CHAPTER / SCENE IV

Clive Wearing. (*to Deborah Wearing*) You're beautiful. Absolutely gorgeous.[51]

Sacks. His passionate relationship with [Deborah], a relationship that began before his encephalitis, and one that centers in part on their shared love for music, has engraved itself in him—in areas of his brain unaffected by the encephalitis—so deeply that his amnesia, the most severe amnesia ever recorded, cannot eradicate it.[52]

Journalist. …Readers, on the other hand, have acquired a taste for trying to ferret out the presence of the author (or his unconscious) even beneath the surface of works which do not look autobiographical, so great is the extent to which fantasmatic contracts have created new reading habits. This global level is

---

[49] Sacks.
[50] Lejuene, 209.
[51] France.
[52] Sacks.

the one on which autobiography is characterized: it is as much a way of reading as a kind of writing; it is a historically variable *contractual product*.[53]

Deborah Wearing. However devastating the damage has been, his soul is absolutely functioning…The very fact that he is so despairing, so much in anguish, so angry, so much in love with me, those are all real human passions. All he shows us is raw human passion, straight from the heart of the mind.[54]

EPILOGUE

Journalist. His first words to her were:

"The most important things cannot be spoken. That's why there's music."[55]

---

[53] Lejuene, 219-20.
[50] Deborah Wearing in *The Mind (Second Edition)—Life Without Memory: The Case of Clive Wearing Story*, Part 2, BBC, https://www.youtube.com/watch?v=ipD_G7U2FcM.
[55] France.

HIDDEN IN PLAIN SIGHT

IRENE VELENTZAS

I am six years old. I am sitting on a couch sunken with age, resigned to its unfortunate state of existence. It's brown, perhaps with grime, and smells faintly of coffee and stale cigarettes. A stooped and wrinkled figure criss-crosses the room gesticulating around his haphazard kingdom. This is my grandfather—an uncanny shrunken image of my father. From the top of a ramshackle wall cabinet he pulls down a dusty old cigar box. I don't see the need to place such an ordinary item so high, out of sight. The small room is filled with all manner of faded and tattered objects, dozens and dozens of them. Empty bottles of every size, shape, and colour are arrayed seemingly without order, the light catching them like a sigh, dust clouds dancing in its beams. I watch and do not speak as he says to my father, "I never want you to worry about money, my son. I have my savings right here. If you ever need money, this is yours." He opens the box and displays wads of crumpled bills.

I'm not sure why my father would need to worry about money, or why he would need my grandfather's old cigar box. I have more pressing matters to attend to. I have to use the washroom. I say so, hesitantly, in Greek. My eyes bounce from my mother and father to the unfamiliar and careworn faces around the room. I'm not sure what to do in this foreign place with these foreign people I'm told are family. My grandmother ushers me warmly: "Come this way, child. I'll show you where it is." I don't really register her face, just her body, warm and enveloping, and sunken, much like the couch whose embrace I've just left. My mother comes with me, and I'm grateful for her company.

We wind our way through an endless warehouse. It doesn't seem much like a house at all, but some other world, filled with mountains of overturned chairs, mats, pots, and other indiscernible items swallowed up by the whole. I've never seen a place so full in my life. I worry about straying off the narrow path that winds through the heaps of cascading broken furniture, which create the only partitions within the large long room, en route towards the faraway washroom. My grandmother stops suddenly in the middle of the path, sighing with the walk's effort, "Here we are." She points to a cracked porcelain pot sitting in the centre of the floor amidst the surrounding bric-à-brac, rank with the contents of human feces. I look up at my mother in confusion and begin to cry.

• • •

"Your grandpa was a good man," my father tells me as we walk along. I can't recall where we are going or how this comes up. "Always, he provided for his family. He said to me one of the last times I saw him: Stelaki, I never want you to worry about money…"

"And he pulled down an old cigar box from the top of the cabinet and showed you where he kept his money," I finish, surprising myself by plucking a moment some twenty-five years old from my memory. I usually finish my father's stories in a neat two-line summary. He doesn't have many, but the few he has I know by heart. They are so long and circuitous with pockets of remembrance, forgetting, and exaggeration, that I cannot bear to live through each new variation. But this is one of those rare times where my father and I speak of something new—a memory we've never broached before.

"Ooooeeee. How you know that? You remember?"

"I was there in Yaya's and Papou's house, and I remember him handing you that box." To be honest, I had never known if it was a recollection or a dream. The memory has an unnatural elongated quality to it, like I didn't see it with my own eyes but through someone else's.

"You see! You know, your papou was always a good man." My father swells up with pride at the humanity of his forefathers, then falls silent once more, satisfied.

I am surprised he doesn't carry on. My father has a flare for the Homeric, telling epic tales which start in medias res and never seem to end; smatterings of heroic trials pepper tales of routine excursions to the grocery store where my father reigns victorious against the hostile masses to bring home the last of the roast chickens. He is the Odysseus of his own imagining.

This is the first time we have spoken of this story, this shared memory. Sharing such memories is such a rarity it stuns me into silence.

I don't mention the bric-à-brac hovel, the filth and rubble that terrified me as a child. That is not the point of my father's memory. So we walk on.

• • •

"Come here, just come here one minute. Look at this. Look at all this!"

There's no not going there. There's no not looking. My mother is in one of her tirades, and understandably so; my father has gone too far yet again in his daily absurdities.

She pulls me into my father's tool room, a small antechamber extending from our home's back entrance. We have just managed to squeeze through the downstairs doorway to the little room by pushing the door against the rubbish stacked behind it. There is room enough for us to stand side-by-side in the opening beyond the threshold and not much more. We survey the rubble, or rather, I survey as my mother continues her rant. In the six feet between our doorway and the downstairs exit is a horseshoe of assorted junk. Along the left wall there is a large wooden tool bench that takes up most of the room. Along the other wall, a red tool cabinet with two tiers of drawers stands beside a full-sized spare fridge. Between these two, piled up against the outer door, is a barricade of assorted items connecting both sides of the room.

I used to worry about this arrangement as a child on days when firemen came to visit my classroom and teach us about fire safety. When we were asked to create escape routes for our homes I always thought about the downstairs door and the unscalable mountain of objects that barred me from escaping in time. How would I ever get out alive?

In the tool room, everything is at your fingertips, if only you knew where any of it was. Above the tool bench hangs an obsolete pegboard, its pegs lined twelve items deep with assorted merchandise arranged with no apparent purpose. Many of the items are still nestled in their original plastics and covered with a fine layer of dust. In front of this wall display, the table is lined with short plastic drawer sets, ideal for screws and nails, bits and bobbins of various sizes; only, it's hard to even see the drawers through the rolls of tapes and measures and bags and books and cans and half-eaten snacks all strewn about the top of the bench. The underside of the bench is no better; I'm not certain even my father knows what's buried under there. Across from this, the drawers of the cherry-red tool cabinet are so pregnant with assorted tools of every kind they do not open or close, the contents of their filing system plainly useless. Even the fridge is not left uncovered, it's top littered as far as the craning neck can see with WD40 cans, spray bottles, and oil jugs in indeterminate stages of emptiness.

"Just look at this!" My mother has abandoned all restraint, tossing various items from the debris, and further fanning her rage.

"One, two, three, four, five, six…" the exasperation is now pouring out of her unbridled, "…seventeen! Seventeen scissors! Who needs seventeen scissors?" She swivels around, diverting her frustration from the pegboard holding all of these scissors to the standing toolbox behind her, "And here! Two more! Just look at this, look at THIS!" She moves on to her next target. "Eight flashlights! Eight flashlights under this bench alone, and who knows how many more? Who knows! He never knows where he has things, and so instead of looking, does he look? Oh no! He goes out and buys another one! *What do you want from me, Sophie?*" She imitates my father's unique blend of innocence and tantrum: "*It was on sale! It was only a couple of dollars. It's nothing!* Nothing? Nothing?" Her wrath builds to a seismic level. "A couple of dollars! I remember a time when we ate meals with only two spoons to share between us, the big one and the little one. He forgets there was a time when a couple of dollars wasn't so easy!"

I stand there, silent through it all, letting the wave of my mother's fury wash over me. What can I say? There is nothing that can assuage my mother's righteousness, and nothing that can save my father from his compulsion to hoard these innocuous items.

The hoarded goods are a perfect spot for hiding contraband. Myriads of chocolates and biscuits, forbidden due to my father's high blood sugar, are concealed in bags of bags within the wreckage.

He also has an unquenchable penchant for footwear. No matter how many pairs he buys he always needs more. This would be fine if he ever wore any of them. Under and over indeterminate piles of objects, we find three pairs of never-worn sneakers, newly purchased. We also find their cardboard boxes. These have been carefully cut into small colourful squares and set next to other piles of scrap paper. When confronted, he can maintain his innocence. *These shoes? I've had these shoes for years!*

I gently release the sigh that's been building. My father knows he's doing something wrong, but he doesn't quite seem to know what it is; he clearly can't stop it and he certainly won't admit it.

"I just don't know what to do. I just don't know what to do." My mother's gaze drops, defeated, her fire and brimstone spent. "What are we going to do with this many scissors? If we get rid of them, he'll just buy more." She glances up at me pleadingly, hoping there's an answer for all of this.

"Donate them to a classroom?"

We never do.

• • •

BEST KIND

Alzheimer's disease   n.

A degenerative brain disease, classified by DSM-5 as a neurocognitive disorder, with insidious onset beginning before 65 years of age, followed by slow development over several years, characterized by dementia called dementia of the Alzheimer type (DAT), loss of memory, and emotional instability, accompanied by post-mortem evidence of amyloid plaques, neurofibrillary tangles, and other brain pathology, usually leading to death between four and twelve years after the onset of the disease. Some authorities believe that the amyloid plaques are responsible for the symptoms and that the neurofibrillary tangles are secondary; others believe that the neurofibrillary tangles are primary and the amyloid plaques are secondary. The disorder is associated with a deficit of the neurotransmitter acetylcholine and may be caused by mutations in mitochondrial DNA, by a defect in chromosome 14, 19, or 21, or by a prion.

Dictionary of Psychology (4th Ed.)

• • •

I am packing for St. John's. The packing process has taken four months already. I've stopped believing it will come to an end. Last time I came back to my childhood home, I hardly bothered to unpack many of the boxes, stacking them here and there around the downstairs living room, making neat horseshoes of books, notes, and the various odds and ends you accumulate when you live alone—like mini spring-form pans for making individualized desserts.

I can hardly remember what I've stuffed in these boxes from my last move, only that I *need* these items. Moving half a country away, when that country is as large as Canada, is a good incentive to reassess the priorities in your life. I have an 8x8x5 foot crate to ship whatever I'll need some 3500 kilometers to my new home. I must be ruthless. I think and rethink every item, every sheet of paper—of which I have at least fifty binders-full—to determine if it will make the cut.

I've donated three large laundry baskets full of books, four bags of clothing, and years' worth of memorabilia and childhood toys to friends and the Salvation Army alike. Now I rummage through my notes, the relics of four degrees. How will I know that I know what I know if I get rid of these papers? What if I need a piece of information flitting on the edge of my memory that only these papers can recall?

The sea of sorting boxes overwhelms me and I get up and wind my way through them as I stretch my legs. I am overcome with weariness. I am overcome with possession and accumulation. I am overcome with the pressing weight of *stuff* that is at once all-important and irrelevant.

I pull out my phone and call my best friend; he's been with my insanity since high school, he'll talk me down.

"Hello?" Ross picks up.

"Have you ever just wanted to corral everything you owned, throw a match onto it, and watch it burn?"

"That bad, huh?"

BEST KIND

I slump on what space remains of the couch. The impact of my body against the leather cushion issuing a squeak of complaint.

"You'll get there," he reassures me.

Maybe I do just need to hear those words. I need to know there's an end to the madness ahead of me.

"You've done a lot, there's a lot of history there."

Is that what this is? History? Is that how I can justify it? I look around the piles of books and papers—the tools of history. A few feet away is a special box filled with pristine notebooks. Beautiful velvet-bound, hardcover, gold-trimmed, blank-page notebooks. I've collected quite a few over the years as gifts or impulse buys, their possibility alluring. I've always fancied keeping a diary, a poetry book, a travelogue. Each time I take one off the shelf and attempt to fill it, I fear marring its beautiful pages. My life is nonsense. I have nothing worth saying or furthermore recording.

"You there?" Ross's voice interrupts the silence.

"Yeah, I'm here."

I look at the empty notebooks. They're coming with me.

• • •

I am sixteen or seventeen years old. I am sitting on a couch, springy yet stiff, a relic of the 1970s but well-preserved. My mom sits to my right.

"Go bring the book, Tasso," she tells my uncle.

My uncle disappears to some back room in his flat, while my aunt busies herself setting refreshments.

My uncle returns and places a careworn volume in my hands. I have heard stories of this book. The hard cover creaks faintly as I open it. To my surprise the pages are unruled. There is a sketch of two people, quite well-rendered with detail, huddled together in folds of clothing, more blankets than anything. My uncle touches the centre of the sketch with a wide, square finger. It takes great restraint not to slap his hand away; his skin's oils deposit themselves on the page, threatening to smudge the sketch upon it.

It is not my book.

"That's not my papou, that's my papou's parents," he says. My uncle takes the other seat on the couch beside me, unaware he has handed me the first piece of family history I have ever known, the first material evidence that I come from a line of people. *These* people, rendered in this fragile book, are my people. I gently turn the page. What I see brings tears so close to the surface I fight not to dissolve.

I have heard tell of my great-grandfather's calligraphy, of his poetic prowess. He wrote in what my mom calls *clear tongue*, a formal type of Greek all but lost to memory now. What strikes me is not the penmanship. Rather, I am struck by the date in the top right-hand corner of the page, May 5, 1884, and the first line of the poem, which bears my name. My name in Greek means *peace*. There's no other word for it. When you say my Greek name, you speak the word for world peace. The first line of the poem loosely translates to "I am sitting under an olive tree dreaming of peace." I close the book and hand it back. A hundred years before he could know I exist, my great-grandfather begins a poem with my name, on my name-day. His namesake, my uncle, is the keeper of this book.

Many years later, my mother will visit Greece and retrieve this book for me. The book's final page is inscribed to me by my uncle, who breaks the chain of custody, not bequeathing it to his own son or grandchildren, but to me.

I am twenty-two when my mom hands me the book and tells me it now belongs to me. We are sitting in the backseat of the car after picking her up from the airport. I am so terrified of hurting it, of ruining it, of losing it to history, that I ask her to keep it locked in the safe.

I want to scan it, and preserve it, and translate it, and keep it in two places at once, before I take responsibility for it.

I have not laid eyes on the book since. I fear it may be lined with silverfish.

• • •

I open the sliding accordion door to the basement and am hit by a wall of methane. I gag. I close the door, march upstairs, and announce, "We have to call the gas company. Something is wrong. I think there's a leak."

My mom and dad are sitting in the early morning light of

the kitchen table, leisurely sipping their coffee. My father wastes no time reaching for his quintessential reaction: denial. "No it's fine. It's just from when they connect the hoses. I don't smell anything."

My mom sits rigid against the gentle curve of the oak chair, her body humming with the effort of restraint. Not twenty-four hours ago did she try to calmly reason with him.

"Now, Steve," she inhaled deeply, "the repair person is coming today to install a new boiler. Please let them do their job, don't stand over them telling them your whole life story, you'll distract them and they might make a mistake."

My dad waved his hand dismissively. "Please, Sophie. Me? I hardly make a *keeh*. I don't bother anyone."

The arrival of the repairwoman, however, presented my father a new and captive audience to regale with the tall tales of his life's adventures. From behind the boiler, the repairwoman's polite laughter drifted upstairs. No amount of my mother's coaxing could entice him to leave the woman to her work.

Later that evening, my mother and I informed my father we could smell gas in the basement, and suggested we call the gas company to come and inspect the issue. My father refused. *He* could not smell anything, so a problem did not exist.

"No." Enough is enough. "If you won't call the gas company, I will! Do you know how dangerous this is? We could all blow up if we flip a light switch!" I exploded at my father, unable to hold my tongue any longer.

Within twenty minutes, yesterday's repairwoman is back at the house investigating the problem. The gas hose has not been coupled tightly enough to the boiler, and has been steadily leaking all night. She's glad we called, it could have been quite dangerous. She advises us to open all the windows, air out the house, and go outside for some fresh air.

My mom paws the ground like a bull before its charge.

Politely thanking her for the umpteenth time with forced levity, my mother gently closes the door behind the repairwoman. Then, she turns, face flushed with fury, upon my father. My father cowers in the farthest corner, simultaneously bracing for the confrontation and running through the rolodex of excuses he has ever-at-the-ready in his head.

"I told you! I told you," she begins quietly, "do – not – talk – to – the repairwoman when she was fixing the boiler!" Her voice crescendos rapidly in the tiny kitchen. "I told you, I told you, you'll distract her! Let her do her job, I told you. I told you I smelt something in the basement, but oh no, it was nothing! Big Steve always knows best! You could have gotten us all killed! Is that what you want?"

She is determined to impress the severity of the issue onto my father. Since I have left home, he is her only companion, her responsibility, her greatest danger. She is the only one to negotiate his constant deterioration, his defiance, his condescension, his severe lapses in judgement. Every moment of every day she navigates the fresh peril he'll unwittingly concoct, for himself and others, and then deny. It's enough to drive the soundest of individuals into madness.

His ever-ready excuses trail off into an incoherent whisper in her wake.

I sit quietly on the stairs, cradling my head in my hands. This is not the first time my father has put us in jeopardy. He loses his keys, his wallet, his direction on a near-daily basis. He leaves appliances on, here, or there, or everywhere. He veers this way and that way on the road, and maintains he's well within the lines. He'll kill us, we tell him. He hears, but does not listen—the ear a useless orifice on the side of his head.

• • •

I am seventeen. My father stands at centre stage of the Epidaurus, an ancient Greek theatre carved into the mountainside.

I have had to fight tooth and nail to see this place. It is the first time I have visited Greece in over a decade. We have whittled away the first two months of our vacation doing nothing in particular. My mom won't wander too far away from home when we go out. It's not our home, and she doesn't know what might happen while we're away, so we never go away. But there are only two weeks remaining of our holiday and I intend to live them to the fullest. I make up an itinerary and my parents agree to see the sights.

I've started a diary for this occasion, and I intend to fill it up with my experiences gallivanting across the ancient Greek ruins by day and dining with family and friends by night. In just ten days I have dragged my parents to see the Acropolis, the Temple of Poseidon, Leonidas's memorial at Thermopylae, the Temple of Athena, the Oracle at the Temple of Apollo, the original Olympic Stadium, and now the first theatre, the Epidaurus. I sear each moment, each monument, into my memory, binding myself to my ancestral home.

Puffing after a three-hundred step climb, I stand at the top of the open-air amphitheatre, at my father's insistence. He's eager to re-enact a moment of personal history from some fifty years ago, when he first visited the Epidaurus as a boy on a school trip.

As I watch my father, my gaze sweeps around the majestic panorama of the wild Greek mountainside below me and along to the perfect concentric limestone rings carved into the mountain enveloping me. An exquisite man-made ear— the ear of the gods listening to the toils of the mortals below on centre stage. My father looks so small from here, rather like the boy he was when he first visited this ancient place. Though he is small, the smile on his face is large.

He fishes out some receipt that's been idling in his pocket, just some inconsequential piece of paper for later discarding. He holds it out before him, pausing briefly, and then in one swift motion, he tears the piece in two.

Riiiiiiiiiipppppppppp...

The sound echoes up the mountain. I hear it as if he's

standing right next to me, ripping the piece of paper beside my ear. A re-creation of the same sound he heard when his teacher stood where he stands and ripped a piece of paper for the class to hear. A sound that has been rippling from the proscenium arch to the ears of spectators for thousands of years. A sound made only to be heard. A sound preserved.

From this great height, I can see the gardens surrounding the theatre's base. The theatre, magnificent as it is, is only one of the many wonders of this place, nestled within the ancient land reputed to be the birthplace of Apollo's son: Asclepius, the healer.

To reach the ancient hand-carved theatre we passed amongst these healing gardens; the delicate pink petals that push themselves out of the rocky earth to sway back and forth in the summer breeze as superb a creation as the ancient stage chiselled into the mountainside. Both are places of re-creation. Both are places of catharsis. The soft perfume of wildflower gardens lingers on the air. The dry, sandy earth intertwines with the fragrant breeze whispering against my skin as it passes, sharing its secrets with visitors across the millennia.

I sit on the topmost step of the Epidaurus. My father moves off stage. I hold his smile in my memory, our shared moment of discovery. I hold the memory of my father's smile, recreating it, revisiting it, until the day comes when I can hold it no longer.

SHE GETS A PAPER ROUTE SO SHE CAN SAVE UP FOR A BICYCLE

MICHELLE PORTER

She tells the bald man who opens the door that she is collecting for the *Sun*. He is four tabs behind, which means he hasn't paid for eight weeks and that is the entire time he has subscribed to the newspaper.

Her little sister jumps up the last step and leans to the left to see if she can get a better view of the insides of the house. Her sister likes looking inside houses. She does too. It's one of the interesting things about going around collecting money for the folded newspapers she leaves in mailboxes six mornings a week.

She likes how the doors open wide for her so she can see just that bit from the front steps because it is like overhearing two of your teachers talking in the hallway when they don't know you're there. She sees so many things. A fat cat on winding stairs; three cabbage-patch dolls in diapers leaning against a big couch; a skateboard sticking out of a neat coat closet; happy shoes in a jumble beside a row of ski boots. Lots of times kids open the door and they have to yell to get their moms or dads and there is a terrific sort of confusion as they swoop in, searching pockets and purses for the right change because she doesn't have enough.

She has to cross the bridge to come to these houses. In the mornings she comes out in the darkness to pick up the newspapers from the corner up the hill and deliver them to the houses that want them, from Akinsdale Street to Belford Avenue. Some of the houses have dogs that bark but most are quiet and still asleep when she leaves a newspaper in their mailbox. One of the houses has a woman who is always awake and complains if she is late so she always tries to make herself get up right away when her alarm clock goes off.

It's usually not so hard to make herself get up because the mornings are this thing she never knew until she had to be outside before anybody else so she could save up for a bicycle. She thinks only the boy who delivers the other newspaper understands. They've never talked and he's already a teenager but he always nods at her and she believes that means he understands about everything.

Every two weeks or so she crosses the river in the hours after school to collect. Soon but not yet the houses will begin to cast

SHE GETS A PAPER ROUTE

their shadows even before she has finished her dinner. On this afternoon, she has already gulped down a bowl of macaroni and cheese and still a stubborn sun hangs onto a sky she doesn't know is big because she's never seen another. The houses are exposed, every line drawn thin and straight.

The man who opens the door doesn't have any hair and he wears the kind of clothes all the men in this neighbourhood wear. The smell of him and his house stings her nose, like the smell of the social-studies teacher who gave her a list of books she might like to read and asked her what she thinks about them even though she is too embarrassed to say what she is thinking to anybody. The man in the doorway smiles. She tells him she is collecting for the newspaper and how much he owes. He fumbles with his wallet and drops it because he is not looking at his hands but at her sister. He makes some silly joke as he picks it up and because they are polite, awkward children they laugh a little without making too much noise. They do this even though what he said wasn't very funny. They do this because they see he has tried to please them and that is enough to make them want to please him in return. The man in the doorway gives her the money and keeps talking to her and her sister. She looks in the direction of the river, of the bridge they just crossed to get to this neighbourhood.

If she stands in the middle of the bridge she can drop a dandelion on one side and watch it come out from the other side of the bridge and the little yellow dot will bob on the water as far as she can see. She imagines it going quite far down the river, beyond the mall, even, and its parking lot. She's never been any farther down the river than that. But upriver she's walked along the path to the library and even as far as Lion's Park. The river bends away there, tearing itself away from the playground, but she has never followed it because she always races her sister to the swings.

The river, it runs like her little brother, bobbing a little bit over the bumps and toddling along for a while then suddenly rushing ahead to catch up with a floating log and hanging back to play over the metal cage of a rusty shopping cart that lies half-in and half-out of the water.

Her sister is with her on the bridge. Which is kind of annoying but also a bit good. Her sister wants to keep standing on the bridge dropping flowers and watching, getting more flowers, and dropping them again. She knows how many doors are waiting for her so she walks to the other side of the bridge.

She is on the hilly side of the bridge calling to her sister to come and she can see the row of brown apartment buildings on the other side. They live on the third floor. Once they lived on the ground floor but that was when they were little and they could just open the back door and go to the playground near the river but their mom didn't like how people would come to

SHE GETS A PAPER ROUTE

the door, come inside anytime if they liked and were always calling through the door, asking "can she come and play?" So now they have a balcony and have to walk downstairs and through the front entrance and walk around to the back to get to the slides and stuff. Anyway, she doesn't care so much anymore. She just leaves when she likes and goes back when it suits her.

From this side the river doesn't look so nice, she thinks. Not with their apartment building there beside it. The apartment building is long and curves in and out in deep scoops. She likes looking over the river from their side because then she sees the river beside the trees and the path that leads up the grassy hill.

Her sister had wanted to bring her She-Ra doll and she had said okay, sure, because it was only a small, plastic thing, it would fit in her hand. She-Ra The Princess of Power is her sister's favourite hero from the weekend cartoons. And now her sister is saying she wants to watch She-Ra float down the river and she is saying no, you'll cry like a baby. Her sister does it anyway, she lets go of She-Ra and watches as the plastic woman tumbles into the water. She-Ra doesn't make much of a splash and she doesn't float like the dandelions. She sinks, which makes her sister bawl so she has to talk mean to her to get her off the bridge, come here now or I'll tell mom what you did. Her sister stops screaming and walks to the end of the bridge, sniffling. She takes her sister's hand and drags her up the hill. She doesn't think much of She-Ra in her short white dress and golden knee-high boots; she doesn't think her powers are very interesting. Super strength and a magic sword for fighting. She likes Anne of Green Gables because Anne can talk a lot and knows how to make friends, which she doesn't. That's a real superpower, she thinks, making friends. She drags her sister up to the sidewalk and past a lot more streets.

The houses here are curious to her. At Christmastime she goes out alone, wandering from block to block to see the lights and some houses are really decorated, like living gingerbread houses with moving reindeer and laughing Santas and sometimes playing music that she hears even when she goes home and her mom is in her bedroom with her boyfriend and the television is loud and her brother is playing Nintendo. The lights are like that too—they stay with her; ignoring everything, she can lay in her bed and see the strings of colour burned into her imagination.

At Christmastime the river down the hill from the neighbourhood where she delivers newspapers is frozen and she takes her sister and her brother out and clears a bit of snow off the ice and they skate but skate isn't the right word for the bigness she feels sliding about on bumpy ice and falling down on mittens and cold knees and holding hands with each other in a line to see how fast they can go which is never very fast because they run out of breath and fall into the snowbanks at the sides. The river is solid at Christmas; it holds them up between piles of snow and won't let anything happen.

Delivering papers those winter mornings is cold and she has to wear two pairs of pants and her legs hurt so bad when she gets back. But there's a still kind of quiet that happens in the frozen darkness. She feels like she's the only one in the world to witness it and that if she keeps walking the houses will all disappear and it would be only her and that winding friend of a river and the trees and something else she doesn't have a word for, something almost like safe or away and now there's almost enough money for a bike. She knows what kind she wants: a mountain bike with wide, rough tires that will take her farther up that river than she's gone before, it doesn't matter what colour.

She is shy but she likes how the doors open wide for her and she has conversations with the houses, discussions that go on long after she has walked away. She doesn't mind how the houses are: some houses are busy and send her away quickly; other houses are slow and like to make a parade of all the people they have in their bellies; with some houses she almost feels like she is being invited to stay a while, but she knows she is never invited; some houses give tips, though she has never been able to guess which ones will and which won't. Dogs don't bother her one bit but her sister stays back on the sidewalk if there is a dog barking and she goes alone to pet the dog and look at the hoard of fruit in the bowl on the table while the boy calls his mom.

What she wants is to get a bike. She has one now, but she got it for her seventh birthday and now her knees hit the handlebars when she rides. She can't use it to help deliver her papers or anything. She can't ride to school or ride around or explore places so she wants to get another one but her mom has trouble buying them shoes for school and if she rips a hole in her jeans or something that's it so she never even asked.

There is one house which looks just like all the others and so she is not on her guard. It has a big driveway and big car sitting in the driveway outside a garage. The path to the house is made of square slabs of concrete and she and her sister jump from one to another—step on a line, break your mother's spine—and the grass is kept short and there is a small row of wilting flowers under the large front window though she will not remember this later. There is a screen door and, behind that, a door that is fancy. All the doors are fancy to her—all shaped fancy or carved with patterns. The doors in the apartment building she lives in are all plain and flat. The only variation is that some of the flat doors have a peephole in the middle of the door, a little watching eye.

It is at this house that the bald man has opened the door. The house behind him is not at all messy and there is a side table

SHE GETS A PAPER ROUTE

with some keys on it and a mirror hung above it and it is like so many other houses she has peered into. The man wears black pants and black shoes and a shirt with a collar. He scoops his wallet from the floor. He pays and gives her a tip. She likes it when she gets tips. She is ready to turn away now, to go to the next house, but the man in the house keeps talking.

He reaches out a hand and he touches her sister's right arm, rubs it slowly up and down.

Then he rubs her arm too, slow and weird and he can see she doesn't like it so he says that there are mosquitoes out, that there was one on her arm. A smile is stuck on her face. She wants to move down the steps and away from this man but her sister is talking to the man. She is frozen by her politeness. Everything goes out of focus and it feels as if the earth is tilted, shifting into a slide that will drop her and her sister into this man's house and she can't hear anything, only the sound of time creaking as it folds itself together.

It is only for a moment and then she can hear the words that are being said and her sister is saying, yes! yes she would like to see the rabbits. They are in the back of the house, in the basement, the man is saying. I keep rabbits, they are cute and fluffy, you must see them and he is looking at her and at her sister and time really is doing that funny thing. She is made only of bikes and stories and rivers but she recognizes the way he is looking at her and at her sister.

BEST KIND

She knows it from the time the man at the church called her mom, said we're going to pick our daughter up from teaching at church camp and would the girls like to come with. And they did because it was summer and there was never anything to do and they dressed as nicely as they could, like for church, because the man was very respected in the church. His wife was with them in the car but she stayed behind while he took them for a walk along a river. He kept looking at them in that way, told them it was too hot for their tights, helped them take their tights off and wanted to twirl them around the way you do with little kids, hanging onto arms and legs, even though they were not so little anymore. But every time his hands went the same way, up their skirts to their panties. So they said—politely, quietly—they didn't want rides anymore and he took them back to the car. They curled their little bodies around each other in the back seat and pretended to fall asleep so they didn't have to talk to him or his wife the whole way home. The next day her little sister told their mom who told their big cousin who talked to the pastor who talked to the respected church man—who admitted that he was attracted to little girls and that he would pray to God for help. After that, they all sat on the opposite side of the church from him. This man is like that church man.

Her feet have turned to concrete on the front porch. She is shy and it is polite to go into the house and see what this old man

SHE GETS A PAPER ROUTE

so kindly wants them to see: she knows that. But she knows that something will happen if they go in the house. Her sister is excited about rabbits and is leaning inside the house and she does not know how to stop everything. The world is tilting and she, too, is sliding through the carved wooden door. Along the way a memory is knocked loose and she grabs hold of it and finds that it is a memory of the future.

She is on the phone with her sister who is an adult and she must be an adult too, though she cannot shake off the feeling of a child's gangly body. Her sister is saying, do you remember? Oh, she remembers. She remembers the dairy farm they stayed on when she was almost thirteen. She remembers the nice couple they lived with, the funny German man and the sweet round blonde woman, his wife. She taught them a little German. He taught them to milk cows. She taught them how to play simple songs on the piano and how to pick onions and tomatoes and chop dill into potato salad. But that isn't what her sister on the phone is talking about. Her sister is talking about the round woman's brother. The round woman's brother was tall and skinny and beige, another man who looks hungrily, who finds excuses to touch in that way that makes her squirm away, stick close to her sister, never leave her alone, never be left alone. On the phone her sister is saying, remember we loved driving that Honda three-wheeler, you on front, me on back, and he was always calling us over but when we went over he would rub his erection against our legs while talking about something else almost like it wasn't happening? You—you refused to go near him anymore, you just ignored him, revved the engine and roared past him as quickly as possible, pretended you didn't hear. And later when the round woman was there to hear he would ask you why you had been rude, and you would just say oh, we had to go somewhere else or oh we didn't hear, so the round woman with blonde hair didn't say anything about it. Remember? He was always saying kids needed hugs, he was always begging for hugs, and at first we tried to pretend not to hear him but when that didn't work and he kept on pressing us against his body in long weird hugs you just said, I don't want to hug you. I remember my heart beat fast the first time you said that because everyone could hear; I was scared of what might happen. I hid behind you when you said that—I don't want to hug you. I didn't say anything at all so they all thought you were the mean one. But I knew you were brave; you were my hero.

This is a revelation to her adult self because she has never thought of herself in that way.

She, always conquered by silence and awkwardness, she who has never been able to begin to master Anne's superpowers, has never thought herself a hero.

There on the steps of that unremarkable house when she is still just a child she hears her sister some thirty years in the future

SHE GETS A PAPER ROUTE

say but I knew you weren't mean at all, you were my hero, did you know that? All of a sudden she feels as though her skinny back has sprouted wings. The slide vanishes; the ground becomes as flat as it has always been. Haltingly, she speaks the lie that comes to her, the lie she must offer even though she is tortured with embarrassment: no, no, we don't have time, our mom is waiting for us. Her sister whines and wants to see the rabbits and the man's hand is on her sister's arm now, but gripping. Our mom, she says, will be mad because she's waiting around the corner, in a car, a green car. The hand on her sister's arm loosens. He looks around. But you'll come back another time, won't you he asks with the kind of smile those men always slide onto their faces. Yes, yes, she whispers meekly, politely, next time. She glares at her little sister as she says this, the look that always makes her listen, and drags her away from the man's grip, away from the open door, down the steps and up the street, past all those houses she doesn't see.

FIREFLIES

HEIDI WICKS

The balmy New Hampshire night drapes a sticky sweat over my face, neck, arms, legs. The stars twinkle above our parked 1987 Brother Boler brand trailer, which is round and short and beige with a thick brown stripe around its middle.

On the highway, whenever we'd pass another Brother Boler, Dad would proclaim, "Look kids!" pumping his fist in the air, "Brother Boler!" and he'd barmp the horn and tip his imaginary hat at our long-lost highway sibling.

The campfire sparks and crackles. Dad makes giant bunny rabbits and owls and hawks fly across the camper with his hands.

"Heidi." There's a tug at the side of my hot pink Much-Music t-shirt. "Let's go hide in the woods and see how long it takes them to find us." Maggie is only eight, a whole year younger than me.

I sigh. "Well okay. But I'm finishing this hot dog first." I twirl my twig over the flames with expert precision until I sense the dog is satisfactorily striped with crisp-black char and globby-BBQ-sauce red. I raise it and examine it by the light of the fire—*nice work, Me*. I blow on it daintily and take a cautious nibble. Maggie is wriggling and holding onto her crotch.

"Do you have to go to the bathroom?" I glance away from the wiener, mid-blow. She shakes her head nuh-uh. "You could go now, while I'm eating. You don't want to pee in the woods." I recall being at the cabin last summer, when I was only eight myself. We'd gone blueberry picking on the wee island across the pond and I'd had to pee, but when I dropped my drawers and crouched, the pee went all over my jogging pants. My grandfather, Goggi, laughed so hard he started choking on his own saliva. I vowed right then and there to spread awareness that crouching in the woods can be unpredictable.

Maggie bolts into our camper to relieve herself, and I turn my attention back to the hot dog, plucking the last bite off the stick. I just finish sucking the sauce off each finger when Maggie bursts from the trailer. *That was fast.*

"Are you ready now?" Her eyes are wide and she's jumping up and down.

"I think Maggie's a bit hyperactive, personally," I'd heard Dad say to Mom when we were driving to the campsite and I was pretending to be asleep.

"John, she's not hyperactive." Mom won't say a bad thing about anyone. But I knew if I could've seen her face, she would've been flaring her nostrils, which was what she did when trying to stifle laughter.

Maggie and I head towards the woods.

My parents and Maggie's parents, Linda and Dan, sit on rocks and fold-out chairs by the fire. Dad sips on a cigar in one hand and a Lamb's and Diet Coke in the other. Dan does the same. Mom and Linda giggle on red wine, and Linda's giggle is high-pitched, twitter-ish, and free. They've known each other since they were five, growing up on Baltimore Street.

"We were called The Baltimore Street Girls, you know," Mom bragged one day as we drove to my flute lesson.

"Gee, that's creative." I'd scoffed from under my perm.

Maggie and I creep through the darkness, our pink jelly-shoe-ed feet snapping twigs on the ground. Not one cloud blurs the crisp crescent moon and glittery silver stars that blanket the treetops. Fireflies zap at each other, their electricity creating sparks in the dark. The soft, thick wind shooshes the forest to sleep.

But we're at a sleepover. The forest is being lullabied, but we're staying up all night.

"Psst!" We jump, startled. I stumble against a tree and scratch my forearm. Maggie scurries into my side.

"Maggie! Over here!" It's Maggie's older brother, Eric. He brought his friend Darren along on the trip. Eric and Darren are both twelve. Their meekly sculpted, albino teenage biceps glow in the dark.

"Eric?" Maggie whimpers and cuddles into me more. I inch away.

"We're right here!" Eric holds his hand out to take Maggie's. He's never mean to her. He's not like most brothers. Zap go the fireflies.

I finally spy him. His red hair is its own campfire and his freckles are speckles jumping away from the main flame. He's smiling. His eyes graze from Maggie's face to mine, and my gaze flits to the forest floor, which looks like it's covered in sawdust or mulch. I kick at something nonexistent.

I hear trickling.

"Jeez b'y, Darren, give it up now." Eric glances behind him.

"A man's gotta go when a man's gotta go." I hear a zipper zip and Darren steps from the darkness, striding like a cowboy. "Had to give him a little shake before I put him back in his house." He winks at me.

"What're you girls doing out here?" Eric has his arm around Maggie, but he's smiling at me.

"We just wanted to go for a walk." I can't maintain eye contact. My armpits are dewy like the morning grass. I think of Tracy Smith from school and how she smells like Cheezies because she doesn't wear deodorant. I hope I don't smell like Cheezies. I try to look like my neck hurts a little bit so I have to turn it to work out the kinks, but really I'm just trying to see if my armpits smell like Cheezies.

"What're your parents at? Drinkin', are they? They gonna

do it tonight or wha'?" Darren holds a twig with his right hand. With his left hand he has formed a circle with his thumb and index finger, and is poking the stick in and out of the circle.

"Darren! Jeez b'y. Don't be at that." Eric tries not to laugh too hard. I try too hard to laugh.

"Do what?" Maggie's knobby knees knock together and her hands are folded in front of her and she's tucked under her brother's armpit. "What're you talking about, Darren?"

Darren cackles and bends over, pretending to wipe his eyes. I chuckle, pretending to have intel on what's so funny.

"Do what? Poor little Maggie, don't know what sex is."

"What's sex, Eric?"

Oh my God. This is humiliating. I can't believe she doesn't know what sex is. Wait a minute—I don't know what sex is, either!

There exists a photo of me on my first Christmas. It's in a white-covered photo album with big rainbow-coloured dots all over it. On the inside cover, 1979-80 is written. There are six square, round-cornered photos on each page, mummified underneath a thin plastic sheet. If anyone were to try to remove a photo from the sticky base they lay on, they'll be destroyed. In this photo, I'm eight-months-old and wearing a red sleeper with a baby-size Santa hat. Eric, age three, is plunked down next to me. His arm is around my shoulder and he is kissing my cheek. I am bawling.

"Look at you and Eric." Mom and Dad say it every Christmas. "You didn't want any part of him kissing you, that's for sure!"

"You knows what sex is, right?" Darren is smirking right at me now.

"Yeah." I lie. Can they see my training bra through my t-shirt? Mom bought it for me at K-Mart just before the trip.

"I can't believe my little girl has a training bra!" Mom pretended to sniff and wipe a tear away. Then she nudged me and asked me if I wanted a Laura Secord French & Frosted Mint.

It could only ever be French & Frosted Mint. All of the other flavours at Laura Secord were garbage in my opinion. SuperKid? Bubblegum Swirl? Pishah. Yuck and yucker. Classless. Heathen's food.

"So who would you have sex with then?"

"Leave her alone, Darren, b'y." Eric is so nice.

"I don't know, probably Jon Bon Jovi." I remembered sleeping over at Maggie's once and there'd been a Bon Jovi poster on her wall.

"It used to be Eric's, but he said I could have it," she'd told me.

Eric's face lit up. "You like Bon Jovi?"

I'm glad it's dark and he can't see that my face is scarlet.

"Yeah. They're cool. I like the lead singer."

"Eric, I'm scared." Maggie. God love her.

"Let's go back guys." Eric. God love him.

When we get back to the campfire, it isn't the only thing

FIREFLIES

that's lit. Our parents are feeling no pain.

Dad stands and creeps over to us. Maggie faces her family's trailer, about to step inside to call it a night. But not on Dad's watch. He creeps over her shoulder and when she turns around he's holding a flashlight under his chin.

"Ahhhhh!" She shrieks and bolts to her father. She hyperventilates and in the firelight I can see the wet spot her tears are making on Dan's muscle shirt.

Dad and Dan went to Woodstock '94 together, years later. At the age of fifteen, I snuck a look at their photos and there were bare-chested women on the shoulders of stoned men, swaying to Joe Cocker and Nine Inch Nails and everything in between. Dad and Dan were filthy in the photos. Dad had on a tie-dyed K-Mart t-shirt and Dan wore a Panama Jack tank top.

"Did you guys smoke marijuana when you were at Woodstock?" I had to know. Dad did this laugh where he'd shoot a series of short exhales through his nose while keeping his mouth shut and allowing no vocals to escape. "Well? Did you?" He never did answer me. He just kept doing that laugh. "You did, I know you did." Puberty: when your allegiances start to drift from your parents to your peers, but you're a bit afraid to fully let go. I wasn't sure if I should be impressed or appalled that Dad smoked weed at Woodstock.

"Thanks for scaring the shit out of my kid, John." Dan hoists Maggie up into his arms, concealing chuckles. "Asshole."

"Maggie, I'm really sorry, I didn't mean to scare you, sweetheart." Dad is doing the nose laugh and Mom pulls him up by the arm, her nostrils the size of quarters.

By now my two brothers are passed out in the camper, dried sweat and fly repellant making their faces gummy. I go into the trailer at the same time as Mom and Dad. We have to whisper so as not to wake the boys.

"What's sex?" I need to know. I can't risk being asked again. I might not be able to manifest such a smooth recovery next time. Mom and Dad pause. They look at each other. They look at me. They look at each other. Mom nods at Dad.

"Well," Dad is matter-of-fact, "it's when a man puts his penis into the woman's vagina."

Thunk. A firefly splats against the screen door.

Silence.

Horror.

Revulsion.

My nostrils tingle.

My throat tightens. Tightens. An invisible fist squeezes it like one of those foam stress balls.

I smell snuffed campfire and kerosene.

Why would a woman allow such a thing?

I can only gawk at Dad. His hand is on Mom's butt.

"I'm going to bed."

They can't hold it in any longer. Dad's nose laugh fountains into full-on ha-ha-has.

FIREFLIES

"Good night." My dramatic departure features two strides to the other end of the ten-foot trailer. Mom and Dad are howling. I'm glad they find my wild discomfort so entertaining.

But that's fine. They'll get theirs.

Years later, they'll catch me having sex with my first serious boyfriend. I'll be in my bedroom and the pizza slice of light from the opening door will creep over our bodies as Mom peers in, not realizing I'm in there.

Time and space will halt.

Her horror will float into the room and swirl with mine until, finally, the pizza slice will get thinner and thinner and disappear.

For a while after that, Mom and I will sail wordlessly around each other, co-existing in the house as we eat, wash dishes, get a drink of water, go up to bed. I'll get a stink eye or two from Dad.

Then, one day, I'll glance at Mom and her nostrils will be flared.

A SKETCH OF STEPHEN

PAUL WHITTLE

Whenever I'm driving by the hospital at night.

Or when I hear about mental illness and the lack of care, or pass someone who is out there on the streets struggling with it, I think about Stephen.

He spoke. He wondered who he was, then he returned to a state of slow-moving grace.

• • •

Sean came and found me on my break. I was in the staffroom reading, of all things, *The Electric Acid Kool-Aid Test*. I worked there for the money. Good money, to pay my way through school.

"Go make up the beds, Pauly-wally-doodle all day," Sean said. He wore cowboy boots. He turned up the country music.

He glanced down at my book.

"They teaching d'at in school? Dropping acid? What kind of course is that?"

"No I'm reading it for fun."

"You drop too much and you'll end up like your uncle."

He went off down the corridor singing *Mamas, don't let your babies grow up to be cowboys*.

The patient he referred to was not my uncle. He simply had the same surname as me. In a place so small, an island, we might have been related, though my parents swore it impossible. I used to read charts when too tired to concentrate on my schoolwork. I was seventeen. *April 13, 1954. Johnny Whittle first diagnosed schizophrenic.* I read he had been raised in Mount Cashel. I wondered if he was born sick or if he *became* sick. On the long-term ward where he'd spent forty years he was well known for being a bit saucy, funny. He said whatever came to his colorful mind. He also sang. The "keepers" would ask him to sing his favourite, *I left my Heart in San Francisco*. Sean loved tormenting him.

Sean would send me off to do a clean-up job, telling me it was good experience for management. "College boy," he'd say. He must have learned the phrase on TV since no one I knew said that; they said university. He'd grown up in the same neighborhood as me, but I felt it likely he'd be working at "the mental" seven days on, four off, for the rest of his life. He took delight in locking a patient away in TQ, Orwell-speak for rubber room, though its walls were not made of rubber. I learned the codes of institutions that summer. TQ stood for

A SKETCH OF STEPHEN

therapeutic quiet. ECG meant shock treatment. Camcolit, the brand name for the chemical lithium. Locked wards were closed wards. What was once named the asylum, meaning a place of sanctuary, was now called "the mental."

One night I was assigned to an open ward. I learned that Brenda, this girl from up the street, had just been admitted on a thirty-day psychiatric assessment. A nurse told me she'd dropped too many mushrooms, but there might have been more to it. Brenda sat watching TV, her eyes looking forward in a frozen state. I found a copy of Neil Young's *After the Gold Rush* with her stuff under the bed as I was sweeping up. On the cover, Neil walking in front of a black fence, everything painted over in some kind of heavy lead. Like the grey sadness that now consumed her. It scared me, for it could have been me, or my brother, or Sean, or anyone else we knocked around with.

TQ rooms were the same as any locked wardroom, except there was a bubble window on the door where you could look in and observe the patient. Like Jacques Cousteau exploring the condition of the mind of the lost soul swimming in the depths of his illness. The room contained only a mattress on the floor and a clean white sheet. When they called a 666 over the PA, which meant a patient was "acting out," Sean took pride in being the first to race over to the ward in question and jump on the patient, taking him by the scruff and throwing him in TQ. To me, acting out seemed a natural reaction. For how could a patient not want to act out against the confines of the institution, act out against the indignities of being there? Act out of the fervor and rage of their sickness? I often asked the nurses and my parents for insights into the *why* of it all. They looked at me as if I might as well have been asking why there were so many shades of grey in the sky. Acting out was a part of their illness. Any incident like this was labelled a minor psychotic aggression and brought a brief visit from an overtaxed doctor who prescribed an increase in meds.

Sean used to play tricks on the patients, making them beg for smokes, or make beds, or he'd rearrange the chairs in the main room so the patients faced away from him and towards the windows. I watched them, all uniquely sick and lost, look out at the landscape. Clouds and cars steadily streamed by, trees blew in the wind, gulls circled and screeched above the river valley in the near distance below the hospital. Most of the patients stared blankly at this scene, for it held no possibility for them.

I might be down the long hall mopping up piss (even now the smell of Clorox brings me back to that place, those long and confined corridors), or checking doors to see if they were locked. Sean would make them walk all the way down to where I stood, telling them I was down there with smokes.

"Keeper, keeper, can I have a smoke?" they'd ask. And I would have to send them back to the common room. Sean watched it all with his feet up on a vinyl chair, smiling. I looked towards the nursing station but the nurses were afraid of him. If they asked him to stop his shenanigans, he'd always have a

A SKETCH OF STEPHEN

reply like, "It gives them exercise." Or if he had turned on the caged TV to watch some hockey game, turned it away from some cartoon that had made some of the patients smile or dance, he'd say they had to learn discipline. If you challenged Sean he'd say, "I was just joking, b'y," or something like that to make you feel you were too serious, too sensitive.

Stephen knew nothing of any of this. He walked into walls; you had to grab him and turn him around. He never resisted anything, but, somewhat like a baby, was docile and welcomed attention. Some of the nurses sometimes held his hand; Stephen held theirs like a cup, gripping it stiffly.

Stephen was beautiful. He had soft features, a delicate way, hair parted perfectly in the middle, what we called a bowl cut when we were kids. When he stood still, so comfortable in his body, with graceful posture and skin that hadn't seen any sun in ten years, he might have been made of marble. The nurses often talked about his perfect hair, soft and thick. Someone joked he would have made a great newscaster.

I did my first string of night shifts, which was euphemized "casual evening rotation." My first few shifts, I would have to pinch myself to stay awake on the ride home. Once I woke up with a patient staring at me through the station window, as if *I* was the one in TQ. When I made it home and got into bed there was always a crow squawking in our backyard, tormenting me into murderous thoughts. As I drifted in and out of consciousness sometimes I thought I was back in the hospital, a patient standing over me with a flashlight, checking in on me the way I had looked in on them, every hour on the hour. A shepherd of the night.

One morning on shift change, while the nurse was up in the station giving her report, Sean ate his breakfast—he took a hefty portion of whatever the patients had—in front of Stephen and the others while they waited and watched. Then he'd torment the patients, stuffing the food down the throat of one poor disabled soul. Whatever monkey in his mind drove him to be cruel I'm not sure, but, unlike the patients, Sean only acted out when he wasn't being watched. Many of the other orderlies had euphemisms for Sean: "hard ticket," "a head case," "tough as nails," "a real man," and so on.

It was hard for the nurses to pinpoint his actions as worthy of discipline. Sean always kept within a grey area of expectations. That the patients were a kind of collateral damage to this… well, they spouted rationales like *it's better than it used to be!*

Stephen was a prisoner of his physical world, like a man wandering blindly, but without the ability to process his other senses. His walk was measured, something like a man sleepwalking. His face was like a bewildered child's, as if lost in the mall, unable to find a single point of reference. The female nursing attendants and cleaning staff sometimes joked they'd like to sleep with him. "He's a sweetie," they'd say. And in this it was implicit, to me anyway, that perhaps their husbands might not be so.

A SKETCH OF STEPHEN

When I worked nights, I would study between hourly patient checks and other duties, or look at the charts the nurses had pulled out, or, if I got too tired, sometimes I would draw sketches of a scene I had witnessed: the housekeeping staff doing a slow and steady sweep of the floor, or a patient standing in the doorway, like a cat that couldn't make up its mind. They were more like doodles, for I was not then, nor am I now, an artist. I was an observer. Stephen's chart: *Diagnosed 1969. Hydrocephalus from brain damage.* I asked Betty Williams, the night nurse about it. She said it was commonly called water on the brain.

Charlie was an older man. For twenty years he'd worked as a trained nursing assistant, up and down the corridors of West 1A. Tender, he treated the patients like they were his children. He had that hail-fellow-well-met way, that kindness and lack of pretension that is sometimes the mark of a man who'd grown up close to nature. Charlie was not easily distracted and prone to melancholy like I was. He was sincere and not resentful of his lot in life. Not at all like the way that Sean and his few devoted deputies were. Most orderlies were neither good nor bad to the patients, they were just clocking time, arriving in trucks full of junks of wood or 2x4s and couldn't wait to leave town when their shift ended. In a small city with soaring unemployment, a good union-paying job was hard to give up.

Charlie was a bachelor. I thought that had something to do with his way. He loved them like children. When I started working on West1a that summer, he brought me around and told me about all the quirks and needs of each patient. When he got to Stephen he had to tell me the whole story over coffee.

"They were both from Ferryland," he said, "d'ey were swimming somewhere up the shore, and the water must have been high for his girlfriend was about to be swept over the falls. He thought so anyway, but she made it to the other shore, while he banged his head off the rocks. His girlfriend, Cathy, drove him to hospital with what they thought was a concussion. For the first few hours he seemed fine, he said he just felt tired."

I pictured the rest of it as Charlie talked. Stephen lying in a hospital bed, Cathy by his side, and then him slipping away further and further from consciousness into the night. Drowning deeper into a state of utter helplessness.

• • •

The nursing attendant staff were all playing cards, the patients all in bed, and the evening shift work done. They'd throw down their cards when they won a hand, calling SCAT! They'd yell and chide the other players. They'd have someone on watch in case the head nurse or supervisor came by the ward for a look, in which case they'd all jump up and go about the ward as if they were busy.

Charlene, one of the nursing students, said, "Paulie-wally's too good to play cards with us." I was sitting on a chair over in the corner, reading.

A SKETCH OF STEPHEN

He appeared in the doorway.

"Hi, my name is Stephen," he said.

Everyone put down their cards. I put down my book. We waited. Only the level sound of the TV news interrupted the silence. Stephen walked across the room and shook my hand. Again, he spoke, "Hi, my name is Stephen." We all stood up in disbelief. I ran down to get the nurse on duty. I said something like, "Stephen's come out of it."

Patricia was like most of the nurses, caring and thoughtful, when not overwhelmed with paperwork and doing meds. She sat with Stephen and tested his vitals, as if this was a physical manifestation of something, some kind of reflex action. When she told him he resided at a psychiatric hospital, his face registered incomprehension. He talked about where he lived in Ferryland and then asked a lot of questions, like an eight year old. His voice was scratchy, like someone who had a bad cold. I'd never heard him talk before that, just make screeching sounds, like a whale mourning for its pod.

The head nurse came by and summoned all doctors on call via the PA.

Code 333. The doctor on call arrived and after a consult with the nurse he decided to have someone watch him around the clock. I sat for a few hours with him until relieved by the next shift. Stephen kept asking questions that were hard to answer. Most about how he'd gotten to where he was.

I waited for him to ask after Cathy, but he never did.

A few days later on a beautiful evening the staff were all sitting out on Muskoka chairs in a fenced-off area of the ward, outside the fire-exit door. Sean had told them they should take advantage of the day, though he knew it wasn't allowed. As the union shop steward, Sean often bragged, "I does what I wants."

"Here comes the untrained genius. Bow down, for he'll soon be a manager."

I broke out my sketchpad and drew the scene in broad strokes.

Stephen sat reading the paper with his legs crossed, posture perfect.

"Pauly-wally doodle all day," Sean said.

Specialists arrived on planes, there were consults and meetings and visitors. All the staff who'd worked on West1A came out of curiosity to see Stephen.

His family and friends lived in a sudden hope they couldn't comprehend.

I'd gotten moved to another ward to cover someone's vacation for the rest of the summer. A week or two later I left on a coffee break to go visit Stephen. I peeked in on him sleeping peacefully. Charlie told me that Cathy had come to visit. Married now with children, she'd gotten as far as the door of the ward and then she'd fled in tears.

A few days later I heard the news from a nurse on my ward. Stephen had retreated into his sleepwalking shell. I walked over to West1a and found the nurse.

A SKETCH OF STEPHEN

"The doctors did their best," she said.

The usual crowd were playing cards in the common room.

"They didn't *want* him coming out of it," Sean said, laying down his cards, "SCAT!"

I found Charlie making beds.

"Don't mind Sean," he said, trying to be an adult for me. I noticed his face, the lines that had furrowed there, shift after shift after shift.

"Maybe the doctors didn't give a fuck?" At least I *recall* saying something like that. I was young, seventeen. I wanted a reason.

Charlie placed his hand on my shoulder as we looked in on Stephen. His eyes were open but he had cocooned back into his old self.

At home that night, I broke out my exercise book and looked at the sketch of Stephen reading the paper. It didn't do him justice.

This all happened the summer of 1979, when "Wuthering Heights," the Kate Bush song, was always on the radio. My girlfriend would sing along to it in the car. "It's me, I'm Cathy, I've come home."

We'd drive out to the cape or some place to sit on the edge of a cliff and stare out at the ocean.

ACKNOWLEDGEMENTS

JOHN ROBINSON BLACKMORE: "*La respiration sacrée*" Copyright© 2018 John Robinson Blackmore. Printed by permission of the author.

BRIDGET CANNING: "Questions and Answers on Flight and Butchery" Copyright© 2018 Bridget Canning. Printed by permission of the author.

EVA CROCKER: "Swimming Pools" Copyright© 2018 Eva Crocker. Printed by permission of the author.

DANIELLE DEVEREAUX: "*Des biscuits*" Copyright© 2018 Danielle Devereaux. Printed by permission of the author.

AMY DONOVAN: "Night Walk" Copyright© 2018 Amy Donovan. Printed by permission of the author.

MATTHEW HOLLETT: "Painting the Curlew" Copyright© 2018 Matthew Hollett. Printed by permission of the author.

MICHELLE PORTER: "She Gets a Paper Route so She Can Save Up for a Bicycle" Copyright© 2018 Michelle Porter. Printed by permission of the author.

ELENA SLAWINSKA: "Pleasure and Other Nutritious Matters" Copyright© 2018 Elena Slawinska. Printed by permission of the author.

JOAN SULLIVAN: "Clive Wearing Writes (and Writes and Writes) His Autobiography" Copyright© 2018 Joan Sullivan. Printed by permission of the author.

IRENE VELENTZAS: "Hidden in Plain Sight" Copyright© 2018 Irene Velentzas. Printed by permission of the author.

PAUL WHITTLE: "A Sketch of Stephen" Copyright© 2018 Paul Whittle. Printed by permission of the author.

HEIDI WICKS: "Fireflies" Copyright© 2018 Heidi Wicks. Printed by permission of the author.

Image on page 90: John James Audubon, "Esquimaux Curlew, *Numenius borealis*," from *Birds of America*. Hand-colored engraving, made between 1827 and 1838.

Photograph on page 92 used courtesy of Matthew Hollett.

The cover and back-cover design of *Best Kind* are an homage to the former Newfoundland Margarine Company.

CONTRIBUTORS

JOHN ROBINSON BLACKMORE is a townie who has lived on both sides of the island. He took a hiatus from his undergraduate program to work as a French Aide at St. Theresa's Elementary. Subsequently, he travelled twice to India, spending most of his time living at an ashram in Tamil Nadu. He's also spent time in California, Utah, and Saint-Pierre. His short story "Lub Dub Funk" won a Newfoundland and Labrador Arts and Letters Award for fiction in 2018.

BRIDGET CANNING's debut novel, *The Greatest Hits of Wanda Jaynes*, was selected as a finalist for the 2017 BMO Winterset Award and the Margaret and John Savage First Book Award. She was raised on a sheep farm in Highlands, Newfoundland, and currently lives in St. John's where she is working on an MA in Creative Writing and a short-story collection currently titled *No One Knows About Us*.

EVA CROCKER is the author of the short-story collection *Barrelling Forward*, which was a finalist for the NLCU Fresh Fish Award for Emerging Writers and the Alistair MacLeod Award for Short Fiction. She is a winner of the Canadian Authors Association Emerging Authors Award. She lives in St. John's with her cats, Pretzel and Poptart.

DANIELLE DEVEREAUX's writing has appeared in *The Fiddlehead*, *Arc*, *Riddle Fence*, *The Best Canadian Poetry in English 2011* (Tightrope Books), and *Elle Canada*. *Cardiogram*, a chapbook of her poetry, is published by Baseline Press. She currently works as communications coordinator for a research project at Memorial University. She is from St. John's.

AMY DONOVAN has an MA in social anthropology from Dalhousie University and is currently working on a novel as part of her MA in Creative Writing at Memorial University. She also works as a guide in Cape Breton Highlands National Park. Her creative work often plays with perspectives that shift away from human worldviews, and considers how nonhumans experience climate change. Amy's poetry has appeared in *Riddle Fence* magazine.

ROBERT FINLEY's publications include *The Accidental Indies*, *A Ragged Pen*, and *K.L. Reich*. He is the Coordinator of Memorial University's Creative Writing Program in which he teaches primarily creative nonfiction. He lives in St. John's.

MATTHEW HOLLETT is a writer and visual artist in St. John's. His collection of poems about photography and seeing, *Optic Nerve*, won the 2017 NLCU Fresh Fish Award for Emerging Writers. Matthew received the 2018 Cox & Palmer SPARKS Creative Writing Award, *The Malahat Review*'s 2017 Open Season Award for Creative Nonfiction, and *The Fiddlehead*'s 2018 Ralph Gustafson Prize for Best Poem. His work has appeared most recently in *Prarie Fire*, *Riddle Fence*, and *subTerrain*.

MICHELLE PORTER is a Métis writer who has called Newfoundland and Labrador home for almost ten years now. She is currently the editor of *The Independent*. She is studying creative writing and teaching journalism. She holds a BA in Journalism and Communications, an MA in Folklore, and a PhD in Geography. She was selected for the longlist for the 2017 and 2016 CBC Poetry Prize.

ELENA SLAWINSKA was born in Genoa, Italy. She studied Ancient Greek and Latin and graduated with a MSc in Architecture and Planning. She moved to New York in 2002, learned English, and had a successful career as an urban planner. In 2009 she met her dashing husband-to-be, Michael, and they came to the island of Newfoundland where Elena ceased being an urban planner. After turning a baby grand piano into a grand desk—hoping to convert words into music—she started to write. In English.

JOAN SULLIVAN lives and works in St. John's, where she is editor of *Newfoundland Quarterly* and contributes cultural articles and obituaries to local and national publications. When she is really lucky she gets to work in theatre too. Her books include *In The Field*, *The Long Run*, and (upcoming) *Game*. Her theatre scripts include *Rig: The Ocean Ranger* and the stage adaptation of Wayne Johnston's *The Story of Bobby O'Malley*, as well as her one-woman show *Your Only Life*, which she has performed in St. John's, Halifax, and Montreal.

IRENE VELENTZAS is a PhD candidate at Memorial University, working under the supervision of Prof. Nancy Pedri. She has an academic background in Psychology, English, and Education and interests in archiving and creative writing. Her doctoral work examines comics' capacity to reconstruct representations of mental illness through autographic narratives. She is currently co-editing a volume entitled *Sexuality and Mental Illness in Comics* and is organizing a special exhibition of original comics art in St. John's, NL, entitled *War in Comics*.

PAUL WHITTLE was the 2013 Winner of the NLCU Fresh Fish Award for Emerging Writers. He has also received Newfoundland and Labrador Arts and Letters Awards for both poetry and prose. His story "Everything Is What It Is" was shortlisted for the 2009 CBC Literary Awards. In 2012 he had a residency focusing on fiction at the Banff Centre. He hopes to publish a book of short stories and is working in multiple genres, including screenwriting, in the MFA program at UBC.

HEIDI WICKS has profiled local theatre, film, and music for *The Telegram*, *The Independent*, and CBC Radio. Through creative writing study at Memorial University, she has written plays, short stories, film scripts, collaborated on two podcast series, and found her writing family in the form of the Naked Parade Writing Collective writing group. Currently completing Memorial's Masters of Arts (Creative Writing) program, her creative thesis is a novel titled *Melt*, which she read from at the 2018 SPARKS Literary Festival, and which she hopes will be published in the not-too-distant future.